"With realism and no little wit, [...] notion of the monastery as he p[...] school of love where members a[...] gentleness, and patience, especially with those who are different. If one stays the course for many decades, however, one might just be 'overcome by admiration for the holy lives lived by others' and find that the monastery has indeed been an initiation into the very life of heaven. Springing from sixty-some years of monastic life, Michael Casey's profound insights on *lectio divina*, prayer, honoring others, and cultivating self-knowledge invite all readers to a deeper encounter with the other—both human and divine."

—Dr. Glenn E. Myers, Professor of Church History and
Theological Studies, Crown College

"In *Coenobium*, Michael Casey successfully demonstrates that the individual search for God and community life are not two disparate elements of coenobitism but are in fact mutually dependent upon one another. The monastic community exists to help its members seek union with God, and the search for God bears fruit in vibrant community. In *Coenobium* Casey speaks directly to those who live monastic life, addressing its realities with wisdom, compassion, humor, and challenge. *Coenobium* contains key insights for monastic communities trying to find a way forward in these uncertain times."

—Colleen Maura McGrane, OSB, Editor of *The American
Benedictine Review*

"This is a beautiful and moving book that opens the inner chambers of monastic and contemplative life, speaking directly to the human heart. In its careful, sensitive depiction of the holy ordinariness of Cistercian community life, which is the ambience for experiencing God and for deepening one's relation to God and neighbor, readers are offered a compelling vision of communal spiritual practice with real significance for our own time."

—Sr. Kathy DeVico, Abbess, Our Lady of the Redwoods Abbey,
Whitethorn, California

MONASTIC WISDOM SERIES: NUMBER SIXTY-FOUR

Coenobium

Reflections on Monastic Community

Michael Casey, OCSO

Cistercian Publications
www.cistercianpublications.org

LITURGICAL PRESS
Collegeville, Minnesota
www.litpress.org

A Cistercian Publications title published by Liturgical Press

Cistercian Publications
Editorial Offices
161 Grosvenor Street
Athens, Ohio 45701
www.cistercianpublications.org

Imprimi potest: Abbot Steele Hartmann OCSO. 12 October 2020.

© 2021 by Michael Casey
Published by Liturgical Press, Collegeville, Minnesota. All rights reserved. No part of this book may be used or reproduced in any manner whatsoever, except brief quotations in reviews, without written permission of Liturgical Press, Saint John's Abbey, PO Box 7500, Collegeville, MN 56321-7500. Printed in the United States of America.

1	2	3	4	5	6	7	8	9

Library of Congress Cataloging-in-Publication Data

Names: Casey, Michael, 1942– author.
Title: Coenobium : reflections on monastic community / Michael Casey.
Description: Collegeville, Minnesota : Cistercian Publications/ Liturgical Press, [2021] I Series: Monastic wisdom series ; number sixty-four I Summary: "Michael Casey combines his observations about the joys and challenges of living in community with an appreciation of the deeper meanings of cenobitic life, taking into account the changes in both theory and practice that have occurred in his lifetime"— Provided by publisher.
Identifiers: LCCN 2021022095 (print) I LCCN 2021022096 (ebook) I ISBN 9780879070670 (paperback) I ISBN 9780879070687 (epub) I ISBN 9780879070687 (pdf)
Subjects: LCSH: Monastic and religious life.
Classification: LCC BX2435 .C31435 2021 (print) I LCC BX2435 (ebook) I DDC 248.8/94—dc23
LC record available at https://lccn.loc.gov/2021022095
LC ebook record available at https://lccn.loc.gov/2021022096

Contents

Abbreviations

ABR	*American Benedictine Review*
CC	Corpus Christianorum, Series Latina
CCCM	Corpus Christianorum, Continuatio Mediaevalis
CF	Cistercian Fathers series. Cistercian Publications
CIC	Codex Iuris Canonici
CICLSAL	Congregation for Institutes of Consecrated Life and Societies of Apostolic Life
CRIS	Congregatio religiosorum et institutorum saecularium
CSQ	*Cistercian Studies Quarterly*
GILH	General Instruction on the Liturgy of the Hours
PL	Patrologia Latina, ed. J.-P. Migne
SBOp	Sancti Bernardi Opera. Rome: Editiones Cistercienses.
SCh	Sources Chrétiennes. Paris: Cerf

Works by Saint Bernard

Dil	*On Loving God*
Div	Sermons on Diverse Topics
Ep	Epistle
Gra	*Grace and Free Choice*
Hum	*The Steps of Humility and Pride*
Nat	Sermon on the Nativity of the Lord
PP	Sermon on the Feast of Saints Peter and Paul

QH   Sermon on the Psalm "Qui habitat"
Res   Sermon on the Resurrection
SC   Sermons on the Song of Songs
Sent   *Sentences*

"The owl of Minerva spreads its wings
only with the falling of dusk."

G. W. F. Hegel, Preface to *The Philosophy of Right*

Introduction

Coenobium or *cenobium* is a Latin word derived from the Greek *koinos bios*, meaning "the common life." It is a term used to describe a monastery of cenobites—monks or nuns who live in a permanent community under a rule and an abbot or abbess. Cenobitic life is more than cohabitation; it inevitably involves interaction. Unlike the Eastern tradition of idiorhythmic monasticism, where everyone follows their own particular grace and inspiration, cenobitic life aspires to harmony and unanimity. These are beautiful concepts, but the attempt to translate them into everyday realities is a lifelong challenge. Partly this is because the community itself is in a state of constant flux, with new arrivals and eventual departures, with different generations emerging into prominence and then fading, and, progressively, with persons of different cultures trying to find a meeting point between their own customs and those of the long-established community.

Today there are many books on monastic spirituality. Sometimes the impression is given that they are addressed to individual readers, offering techniques by which their spiritual life may be upgraded. It may seem as though living in community is marginal to the main thrust of spiritual endeavor and that the best things in the spiritual life are the outcome of one's own fidelity. Bearing one another's burdens with the utmost patience becomes no more than individual virtue—not allowing the idiocies or demands of others to distract us from our spiritual pursuit.

Perhaps there is a value in approaching matters from the viewpoint of community life, since all the valuable recommendations that we find in these books can be summed up in a dynamic attachment to an evolving tradition and to a community as it passes through all the changes that are typical of real living in a changing world. Participating fully in community life will teach us all the virtues—maybe that is why so many monastic authors refer to community life as a school. There is a theological basis to this. The author of the Epistle to the Ephesians stretched his vocabulary to describe our true situation as Christians as co-heirs in a co-body and co-sharers in Christ's promises: *sunkleronóma, sússoma, summétocha* (Eph 3:6). Our corporate identity is not something accidental added to our personal vocation. We become most fully what God intends us to be by becoming most fully and deeply united with those around us. It is really a corollary of the Second Commandment.

After more than sixty years in a monastic community, I have decided that it may be useful to set down some of my thoughts on how the ideals of communal monastic living are expressed in practice. Inevitably what follows will reflect my experience in my own community, but the result is more expansive than that. I have had the opportunity of visiting many communities of monks and nuns throughout the world, and speaking with many different people about their experience of life in a monastery. Some of the examples I give are drawn from this wider acquaintance, though they have been leached of all identifying characteristics. Others, following the example of Saint Bernard, are no more than exaggerated caricatures, creatures of my imagination, offered to illustrate a point—though these often have a basis in reality (*ens rationis cum fundamento in re*). Any who think they recognize themselves in what I have written should take heart. They are not alone. There are others who share what they thought was unique to them.

Writing a book like this is a challenge from the point of view of exclusive language. Some see as a solution the use of the adjective *monastic* as a noun to cover both nuns and monks. I have avoided this option as reductionist. It is my observation that although nuns and monks are heirs of the same tradition and live under the same rule, the dynamics of daily life are different, and, as far as I am concerned, *vive la différence*. I use inclusive terminology when I believe that what I say applies equally to nuns and monks. There are two reasons that I sometimes restrict myself to masculine references. One is when I am treating of the Rule of Saint Benedict and other monastic sources that have a masculine community as their immediate context. The second is when, in my experience, what I say applies only to monks; it may also apply to nuns, but I do not feel myself in a position to assert this. If the cap fits, wear it.

There are those who would prefer a more lyrical and theological exposition of the joys and meaningfulness of monastic community, perhaps in the manner of Baldwin of Forde. I have chosen not to follow this path but to plot a more down-to-earth course, recognizing the many challenges involved in community living. The reason for this is simple. One of the first hurdles the monastic candidate encounters is confronting the manifest imperfections of the different members of the community that was previously supposed to be a school of perfection.[1] I want to affirm the value and the beauty of ordinary and imperfect communities, and to make the point that they don't have to be glamorous to be worthwhile.

In fact, nobody in their right mind would ever speak of a monastic community in terms of perfection. The more traditional designation is that it is a school of love. And it is clear from the Rule of Saint Benedict that the principal means of expressing that

1. Isabelle Jonveaux, "Internet in the Monastery—Construction or Deconstruction of the Community?" *Heidelberg Journal of Religions on the Internet* 14 (2019): 62: "Furthermore, in an investigation I conducted into the image young Catholic people have of monastic life, community life was the most frequently mentioned positive dimension of monastic life (34.4%). Interestingly, it was also the third most frequent response (18%) to a question addressing the perceived negative dimensions of monasticism (Jonveaux, 2018b, pp. 144–146). This suggests that community life in a time of individualism is sought out by young monastics when they enter monastic life, but at the same time represents a challenge for them."

love is through forbearance; we are called to tolerate bodily and moral weaknesses with the utmost patience (RB 72.6). That faults and failures exist even in Saint Benedict's monastery is indicated by the fact that he devotes twelve chapters to dealing specifically with wrongdoing. The Statutes of the Cistercian General Chapters, over the nine centuries of its existence, indicate that there are few vicious tendencies that have not sometimes found expression in particular cases.[2] These may be exceptions to the rule, but they indicate that when the ancients spoke of monastic life as spiritual warfare, they knew what they were taking about. In warfare, nobody ever has the upper hand in every single battle.

Homo sum, humani nihil a me alienum puto: "I am human and I consider nothing human to be foreign to me." This maxim of the Roman poet Terrence can be applied to a monastic community. The celebrated *humanitas* of the Benedictine tradition does not limit itself to the desirable qualities of the human condition. The impress of sin is not absent. Quirkiness is not banished. Monks are not pious clones. The beauty of a monastic community is shown most powerfully in the tenderness it extends to those who are weak and struggling—as the example of Saint Aelred of Rievaulx illustrates.

Yes, the first close-up and in-depth encounter with a monastic community may reveal attitudes and activities that seem inconsistent with the ideals of monastic tradition, but often these do not, in the last analysis, amount to much. Yes, there are occasional and even systemic scandals, and some of these might become notorious. These must be dealt with effectively. But in the commonality of monastic communities that I have encountered, there is a vast reservoir of goodness and kindness, the result of people going about their ordinary and obscure occupations graciously and without much trumpeting.

---

2. See Michael Casey, "The Three Pillars: Filiation, Visitation, General Chapter," *Analecta Cisterciensia* 70 (2020): 373–403.

I am so convinced of the overarching value of monastic community that I have little hesitation in sometimes lifting the carpet to discover what is underneath. Nearly all monasteries—if they are healthy—generate one or two or more characters who may be termed "eccentric." These people are the treasures of monastic life, living signals that lifelong discipline does not crush liveliness of spirit but seems rather to encourage a certain originality—always, of course, tinged with good humor. They may well be a source of exasperation to those fussy people who want to convert monastic life into a well-run business, but to the ordinary rank and file members they add a note of cheerful resistance to an otherwise orderly life.

It has been said that one of the struggles most of us face is to convince ourselves that we are normal. One of my hopes in looking directly at some of the unmentioned aspects of monastic community alongside its sincere aspiration to goodness is to help readers come to the conclusion that the community in which they live suffers from that most unfashionable of human characteristics: normality. May they continue to do so.

1

Community as Church

Those of us who live in a monastic community quickly learn to develop a tolerance for all sorts of odd behavior. We understand that in a community, as in marriage, there is room for a lot of give and take, that we cannot hope that things will be decided always as we wish, and that what is self-evident to us is often unaccountably obscure to others. When we think about community it is usually the trivialities of daily interaction that take center stage.

As for our own behavior, mostly we follow routines, some personal, some communitarian. We don't think much about fundamental principles but try to develop ways of acting that enable us to live with a minimum of friction and without the necessity of constantly having to review options and to make definite choices. Today is pretty much like yesterday, and tomorrow will probably be no different.

Good habits are a great benefit, because they mean that we can live a moderately virtuous life without having to think too much about either the theory or the practice. There is, however, a downside to this. It is easy for settled routines to become so stale that participation in them becomes listless and perfunctory. *Totum constat de consuetudine, de dulcedine nihil.* "It is all a matter of routine; of sweetness there is nothing."[1] From time to time it may be worth-

---

1. Bernard of Clairvaux, SC 9.2; SBOp 1:43.

while to rekindle our interest in one or two aspects of our monastic observance where some improvement seems possible, so that our life may be just a little bit sweeter than it is at the moment.

To do this efficiently requires that we step back from the details of daily living and consider some of the more foundational truths about our monastic vocation. So, on the understanding that nothing is as practical as good theory, I would like to begin my reflections on monastic community at the level of theology, approaching the community as expressive of the mystery of Christ's church, mindful that, in the Middle Ages, a monastery was often referred to simply as an *ecclesia*. A monastic community was regarded as a particular local embodiment of the universal church.

The monastic tradition does not define a community by the works that it does.[2] This includes the liturgy, the Work of God, "to which nothing is to be preferred." Monks are not canons. The importance of the Liturgy of the Hours derives from its providing an opportunity for the realization of the primary purpose of the monastic life. Historically this has been defined as "seeking God," understood more specifically, since the time of the Desert Fathers, as growing toward an ever more conscious state of continuous prayer. Here, however, it is important to clarify that such prayer is more a matter of actualizing our relationship with God initiated at our baptism than of a specific activity, such as is promoted in meditation workshops. Prayer is not so much a task to be accomplished as a state into which we are drawn—over the course of a lifetime. Prayer primarily involves becoming more mindful of this supernatural reality. It is more than engaging in some facilitative tasks, important though these may be. Growth in mindfulness is both qualitative and quantitative—it involves an ever deeper and

---

2. "The real mission of Benedictine monasticism is to preserve the priority of community life, not out of self-interest but because love—that is, lived fellowship—alone is credible" (Luigi Gioia, *Saint Benedict's Wisdom: Monastic Spirituality and the Life of the Church* [Collegeville, MN: Liturgical Press, 2020], 7). The Benedictine monastery is meant to be a sign and a prophecy of what the church is.

more intense comprehension of spiritual reality, and its gradual expansion into more minutes and more hours of more days.

Such considerations lead us in the direction of concluding that the essential function of the monastic community is to lead and support those who enter in their journey to a closer union with the God who has called them to this way of life. The dynamism of the community is first directed inwards—to animate, energize, and guide its members in their spiritual pursuit and, by its effectiveness in so doing, to equip them to participate in communal activities, in and for the community and for those whom the community serves.[3] The Cistercian monks of Tibhirine were engaged in a mission of evangelization not by preaching the Gospel from the rooftops but simply by striving to live an integral community life, bearing one another's burdens with the utmost patience, and placing no boundaries on the respect and honor shown to others.

It is the interior call of God that is the foundation and heart of monastic community—the vocation given to each member is the source from which all cohesiveness must flow. The initiative of establishing a monastic community—or of allowing it to flourish—remains with God. This is the point made at the very beginning of the Vatican document on the essential elements of religious life. Consecration is the basis of religious life. By insisting on this, the church places the first emphasis on the initiative of God and on the transforming relation to God that religious life involves. Consecration is a divine action. God calls a person who is thenceforth set apart by a dedication to a particular form of life.[4]

This is the point made repeatedly by Dietrich Bonhoeffer in his 1927 dissertation, later published as *Sanctorum Communio.* Anyone can readily perceive the sociological reality of the church,

---

3. "It is contemplation and not the common life that seemed to the ancients to be the ultimate goal [of monasticism]. Their deepest preoccupation was not the union of men among themselves but the union of each with God" (translated from Adalbert de Vogüé, "Le monastère, Église du Christ," *Commentationes in Regulam S. Benedicti,* Studia Anselmiana 42 [Rome: Herder, 1957], 46).

4. CRIS, *The Essential Elements of Religious Life* (1983), §5.

but its underlying theological reality is not visible to our ordinary gaze; it is perceptible only to faith:

> The confusion of community romanticism with the communion of saints is extremely dangerous. The communion of saints must always be recognized as something established by God . . . . It is thus willed by God "before" all human will for community. . . . It is only through faith that the church can be grasped, and only faith can interpret the experience of communion that necessarily arises as evidence of the presence of the church. Man "experiences" only the religious community, but knows in faith that this religious community is "the church."[5]

On this understanding, there is a spiritual quality to religious community that transcends its visible functions—including those performed in the name of the church and for religious purposes. "The monastery is an expression of the mystery of the Church."[6] It shares some of the Church's visibility, but it is also a participant in its mystery.

The spiritual nature of the monastic community is indicated by the traditional ritual of solemn profession.[7] This contains two elements. The first is the taking or making of vows by which the candidates dedicate themselves to God by a specific act of commitment to the monastic way of life, promising a lifelong acceptance of its observance. This is complemented by a second element: the rite of consecration or blessing, by which the celebrant, in the name of the church, consecrates the newly professed. The former element

---

5. Dietrich Bonhoeffer, *Sanctorum Communio*, trans. R. Gregor Smith (London: Collins, 1963), 195–97.

6. Constitutions and Statutes OCSO, 3.4.

7. See Michael Casey, "Sacramentality and Monastic Consecration," *Word & Spirit: A Monastic Review* 18 (1998): 27–48. Reprinted in Michael Casey, *An Unexciting Life: Reflections on Benedictine Spirituality* (Petersham, MA: St Bede's Publications, 2005), 263–85.

by which persons offer themselves is termed "active consecration," the latter is regarded as "passive consecration." As the church is constituted by persons who have been baptized, the monastic community is constituted by persons who have received, in addition to their baptism, monastic consecration. Monks and nuns are set apart and endowed with a sacred character. It is a convocation. All alike have been called by God—otherwise their association with the community will always be fraught by difficulties. This is the point of which Saint Bernard reminds his community:

> This community is made up not of the wicked but of saints, religious men, those who are full of grace and worthy of blessing. You come together to hear the word of God, you gather to sing praise, to pray, to offer adoration. This is a consecrated assembly, pleasing to God and familiar with the angels. Therefore, brothers, stand fast in reverence, stand with care and devotion of mind, especially in the place of prayer and in this school of Christ where the Spirit is heard (*auditorium spirituali*).[8]

The essential holiness of the community means that the monastery becomes a "cloistral paradise"—it is the ante-chamber of heaven and, in an imaginative aside, Bernard notes that it is cohabited by angels:

> Walk cautiously, since there are angels everywhere: according to the commandment given them, they are in all your ways. In whatever room you enter, in whatever corner you sit, have a reverence for your angel.[9]

To explore the nature of a particular religious community, we need to be open to listening to the ongoing vocation stories of its members—these embody the mandate given to the community.

8. Bernard of Clairvaux, *Sermon for St John the Baptist*, 1; SBOp 5:176.
9. Bernard of Clairvaux, *Sermon on Psalm 90*, 12.6; SBOp 4:460.

Such stories are more than narratives about the past. There is a certain plasticity about vocation that allows it, while retaining the memory of an initial experience, continually to reframe itself in terms of the present. As a result, conscientious contributions to community discussions are not merely intellectual judgments, but attempts to formulate a response to an issue in terms of one's personal sense of call, often described as "God's will." In discerning between options, I try to gauge which of them corresponds most closely to what I sense is the ongoing guidance of this inner voice. Instead of defining a monastic community by the activities by which, in years past, it formulated its identity, there needs to be an attentive listening to what the Spirit is saying to the churches today, through the experience of those who have been graced to commit themselves to this way of life.

Vocation is not just a trigger that motivates a person to enter a community. It is a lifelong indicator of the way ahead. Without this inward compass, people will be floundering all their lives. Ancient monastic tradition manifests an awareness of the danger of giving candidates a too-rapid entry into the community—obstacles were placed in their paths so that they would be forced to scrutinize their motives and thereby attain a greater purity of intention. By eliminating worldly and unworthy ambitions, it was hoped that a greater reliance might be placed on the work of grace operative in the experience of vocation. A similar conclusion might be drawn about admitting candidates to solemn profession or to ordination—advancing too quickly may inhibit genuine discernment and may be one of the causes that many leave a year or two afterwards. Often candidates are so anxious to take the next step that they are reluctant to take time for a deeper discernment. Such a delay is time well spent.

This is, no doubt, why Saint Benedict greets a priest aspiring to join the community with the words Jesus addressed to Judas: "Friend, for what purpose have you come?" (RB 60.3). Candidates are expected to possess a degree of spiritual literacy that will enable them to discern by what spirit they are being led. The community also needs continually to ask itself a similar question, seeking answers not in juridical documents but in the hearts and consciences of its members.

Saint Benedict makes the point that God *often* reveals things to the younger and newly arrived members of a community that are unrecognized by the established group of seniors (RB 3.3). The same attention needs also to be paid to visiting monks who are not part of the local community (RB 61.4). Outsiders often see more clearly what inspires a group than those immured in habitual practices. As do those who, for one reason or another, find themselves on the margins of the community. Those caught up in the administration of the community often choose not to see the ambiguities and inconsistencies evidenced in its day-to-day behavior. This reluctance to intervene is a serious abrogation of pastoral responsibility, and it is probably more frequently found in men's communities.[10]

The principle is that the community exists to service the vocations of those who are its members. This obviously applies to newcomers, but it is also true of those who have spent many years in the community. It is, perhaps, less recognized that there is a corresponding responsibility laid on those to whom the governance of a community is entrusted. They need to monitor the deep aspirations of all, and seek to respond appropriately. The

---

10. "The Abbesses tend to be very personal in their relationship to their nuns. . . . They want to know everything that goes on in their houses and to be consulted about all arrangements. . . . The Abbots on the whole seem to be less personal and more distant from their monks. . . . The Abbots don't expect to know everything that is going on in the house and sometimes they are woefully ignorant of how the monks are spending their time" (Ambrose Southey, *Minutes of the General Chapter O.C.S.O: Feminine Branch* [El Escorial, 1985], Appendix I: "Conferences of the Abbot General," [6]–[7]). Reportedly, Abbot Maximillian Heim of the large abbey of Heiligenkreuz in Austria consults his monastery's webpage every day to find out what is happening in the house. See Isabelle Jonveaux, "Internet in the Monastery—Construction or Deconstruction of the Community?" *Heidelberg Journal of Religions on the Internet* 14 (2019): 65.

community exists for the sake of its members and not the other way around. No matter how laudable or necessary its social goals, the spiritual good of its members always has priority. Pope Francis writes, "Growth in holiness is a journey in community."[11] The converse should also be true: growth in community is also growth in holiness.

Seeing the monastic community primarily in terms of its being an image of the universal church leads to its identifying—aspirationally, at least—with the primitive community portrayed in the Acts of the Apostles. We find this linkage at many points in monastic tradition. Basilius Steidle asserts, "The first Church of Jerusalem was the model that Pachomius (+345), Basil (+379), Augustine (+430), and Benedict (+547) never lost sight of while writing their rules."[12] Although he gives only a qualified assent to this suggestion, Adalbert de Vogüé adds that the thesis of the monastery as church "offers to the theologian the best definition of the monastic community, a holy society that is exclusively turned towards God, a society of persons given to one another in love."[13]

Here it is necessary to offer a clarification. A monastery is not a church in the same sense that a diocese under a bishop may be considered a local church. This is, perhaps, more obvious regarding priestless communities. For its sacramental life every monastery remains dependent upon the broader ecclesial institution. The monastic community remains always a lay grouping, even though some of its members may receive priesthood from the bishop, and abbots may trot around wearing miters and wielding croziers. More loosely, the community may be seen as an embodiment of the church in so far as it is an intentional gathering of the faithful,

---

11. *Gaudete et exultate* §141.

12. Basilius Steidle, *The Rule of Saint Benedict with an Introduction, a New Translation of the Rule and a Commentary, All Reviewed in the Light of an Earlier Monasticism*, trans. Urban J. Schnitzhofer (Canon City, CO: Holy Cross Abbey, 1967), 9.

13. Vogüé, "Le monastère," 27.

living in accordance with the gospels and tending to the eternal life that they proclaim. The internal dynamic of such a community is marked by unity in faith and love and practice. It is a communion of disciples. Saint John Cassian saw monasticism not as being a distinct part of the church, or a miniature church in itself, but as a particular embodiment of the church, especially in its aspect of seeking the perfection of charity in holiness of life.[14]

There is a certain utility in insisting on the ecclesial character of the monastic community, since it reduces the possibility that, in some way, the community is understood as the master of its own destiny—free to decide in what direction it should travel and by what means its goal may be realized. The monastic community derives its origin from the call of God; this means that its spiritual purposes have priority over any temporal good works in which it may find practical expression of its discipleship. This was a point made by Cardinal Braz de Aviz at the Abbots' Congress in 2012: sometimes "we must have the courage to diminish our works to save our charism."

Saint Augustine uses the texts from Acts to support an appeal to his companions living a quasi-monastic life in the bishop's house to renounce private ownership.[15] He insists that it is by the renunciation of goods that the group will be able to become like the community in Acts, being of one heart and one mind. The same connection had been made at the beginning of his Rule, written about 397:

> Before all else, live together in harmony (*unanimes*), being of one mind and one heart on the way to God. For is it not for this reason that you have come to live together? Among you there can be no question of personal property. . . . For this is what you read in the Acts of the Apostles: Everything

---

14. See Adalbert de Vogüé, "Monachisme et Église dans la pensée de Cassien," in *Théologie de la vie monastique* (Paris: Aubier, 1961), 213–40.

15. *Sermons* 355–56, dated 425–426; PL 39:1568–81.

they owned was held in common, and each received whatever he had need of.[16]

Saint Bernard makes the same linkage between the renunciation
of private ownership and unity of heart:

> The monastic order was the first order in the Church; it was
> out of this that the Church developed. In all the earth there
> was nothing more like the angelic orders, nothing closer to
> the heavenly Jerusalem, our mother, because of the beauty
> of its chastity and the fervor of its love. The apostles were
> its moderators, and its members were those whom Paul often
> calls "the saints." It was their practice to keep nothing as
> private property, for, as it is written, "distribution was made
> to each according to need." There was no scope for childish
> behavior. All received only as they had need, so that nothing
> was useless, much less novel or exotic. The text says, "as
> each had need": this means with regard to clothing some-
> thing to cover nakedness and keep out the cold. . . . I don't
> imagine they would have cared much about the value and
> color of their clothes. I don't think they would have bothered
> much about them at all. They were far too busy with their
> efforts to live in harmony, attached to one another and ad-
> vancing in virtue. So it is said that "the company of believers
> was of one heart and one soul."[17]

Inequitable distribution of monastic resources is a fundamental
impediment to unity of heart. It is not only that some receive more
goods than others. Often the possession of more personal items
or ones of higher quality indicates that the owner belongs to the

16. *The Rule of Augustine,* 1.2–3, trans. Raymond Canning (London: Darton,
Longman & Todd, 1984), 11–12.

17. Bernard of Clairvaux, *Apologia,* 24, trans. Michael Casey, CF 1 (Spencer,
MA: Cistercian Publications, 1970), 61; SBOp 3:101.

elite in the community, one of a group of insiders clustered around a superior who is a cut above the common herd.

As a holy community, the monastery is pledged to pursue unity of heart and mind. It is not just a sociological unit or an intentional grouping. Quite the opposite: its members will often be drawn from different countries and cultures, from different social classes and educational levels, and from different backgrounds. "There is to be no favoritism, since whether we are slaves or free, we are all one in Christ, and under the one Lord we all take upon ourselves the same service" (RB 2.20).

Saint Aelred of Rievaulx saw the harmonious cohabitation of vastly different brothers as the fulfillment of Isaiah's prophecy about the lion and the lamb living together in peace:

> Consider how God has gathered you together in this place, from vastly different regions and from different lifestyles. One of you, when he was in the world, was like a lion, who despised others and thought himself better than them because of his pride and riches. Another was like a wolf, who lived from robbery, whose only interest was how to steal the property of others. A leopard is an animal marked by variety: such were some of you [who lived] by your wits, through deception and fraud. Furthermore, there were many in this community who were foul because of their sexual sins. Such as these were like goats—because goats are foul animals. There were some of you who lived innocent lives when you were in the world; they may well be compared to lambs. There were others who were like sheep because you lived a simple life. Look now, brothers, and see with how much concord and peace God has gathered all these into one common life. Here the wolf lives with the lamb; he eats and drinks with the lamb and does him no harm, but loves him greatly.[18]

18. Aelred of Rievaulx, Sermon 1.33–34; CCCM 2a:10–11.

Baldwin of Forde went one better. He understood the common life as a participation in the shared life of the Blessed Trinity. In his sermon on the common life (*De vita communi*), he understands monastic community as drawing its origins from the apostles and, beyond them, from the angels, and beyond them from the very being of God:

> It is by no slight or mean or ordinary authority that the institution of the common life is supported and sustained. The primitive church was built on the common life, and the infancy of the new-born church began with the common life. It is from the apostles themselves that the common life has received its form and expression, its title of honor, the privilege of its high position, the testimony of its authority, the protection which defends it, and the foundation of its hope. . . .[19]

> The common life was instituted by celestial models: it was brought down from heaven and adopted by us from the heavenly way of life of the holy angels. . . .[20]

> The common life, then, is a sort of radiance from the eternal light, a sort of emanation from the eternal life, a sort of effluence from the everlasting fountain from which flow living waters, springing up into eternal life. God is life. The holy and indivisible Trinity is one life. The Father is not one life, the Son another, and the Holy Spirit a third, but these three are one life. Just as they have one common essence and one common nature, so they have one common life.[21]

19. Baldwin of Forde, *Sermo de vita communi* 1; trans. David N. Bell, *Spiritual Tractates II,* CF 41 (Kalamazoo, MI: Cistercian Publications, 1986), 156; CCCM 99:229.

20. Baldwin, *Sermo de vita communi* 3; CF 41:157; CCCM 99:229.

21. Baldwin, *Sermo de vita communi* 4–5; CF 41:157–58; CCCM 99:229–30.

Baldwin does not remain in the clouds permanently—he sees the high character of the common life as carrying with it corresponding obligations. Those who embrace this manner of living are bound vigorously to pursue unity, to reflect in some earthly manner the unity of the Trinity. This is to be accomplished, above all, by the rejection of the practice of private ownership:

> This is the law of the common life: unity of spirit in the charity of God, the bond of peace in the mutual and unfailing charity of all the brethren, the sharing of all good that should be shared, and the total rejection of any idea of personal ownership in the way of life of holy religion (*sanctae religionis propositum*).[22]

Seeing the monastic community as an ecclesial reality provides a mandate for three aspects of the life of the community:

a. An insistence on the importance of the sacred liturgy: "nothing is to be preferred to the Work of God."

b. The enshrining of the Scriptures as the basis of the community's shared beliefs and values, and the commitment to living a Gospel lifestyle.

c. Giving priority to the spiritual flourishing of the members of the community as the basis of any external activity in which they are involved.

Let us examine each of these areas in a little more detail.

a. The monastery as church will be characterized by good liturgy. "Sharing the word and celebrating the Eucharist together fosters fraternity and makes us a holy and missionary community."[23] In particular, an ecclesial community celebrates the Eucharist. This

---

22. Baldwin, *Sermo de vita communi* 57; CF 41:177; CCCM 99:243.
23. Pope Francis, *Gaudete et exultate*, §142.

is more than a matter of attending Mass. It is important that the members of the community are able to own what they celebrate as expressive of their life and aspirations. No doubt Saint Benedict's chapter on priests (RB 62) can be read in this context.[24]

We all know from experience that good liturgy requires more than smoothness of ceremonial. It demands a substantial investment of time and resources if it is to be kept fresh and relevant to the changing situation of the community. In the case of some of those entering the community, basic catechesis may be necessary, as well as a training in ritual. But good liturgy involves more than professional performance; it requires a certain receptivity among the participants. It presupposes the possibility of living a recollected and reflective life, buttressed by a degree of silence and the opportunity for *lectio divina*. For a community that is overworked or otherwise deprived of leisure, the liturgy will become an im-

---

24. A problem arises with women's communities who have to rely on a roster of visiting priests for their celebration. There are four possible solutions to this. a) The most obvious one is to have some members of their community ordained. The Vatican regards it as dangerous even to think about such an option. b) The second is to move toward unisex communities in which priesthood would be seen as a ministry within the community, not necessarily associated with governance. I have raised the possibility of ungendered communities in "Towards the Cistercian Millennium," *Tjurunga* 54 (1998): 57–67, and in "Thoughts on Monasticism's Possible Futures," in Patrick Hart, ed., *A Monastic Vision for the 21ˢᵗ Century: Where Do We Go From Here?* MW 8 (Kalamazoo, MI: Cistercian Publications, 2006), 23–42. Such an arrangement is not unknown in history. c) The third option is for a live-in chaplain to become almost a member of the community for all practical purposes, except for juridical status. d) Finally, to make the most of present possibilities by the careful choice of celebrants and the diligent cultivation of their interface with the community. See Conference of American Benedictine Prioresses, *Of Time Made Holy: A Statement on the Liturgy of the Hours in the Lives of American Benedictine Sisters* (Madison, WI, 1978), §40: "The integration of the Eucharistic celebration within the liturgical life and experiences of the community is an essential element of Benedictine Christological spirituality. The selection of ordained celebrants and community liturgists who will make joint efforts to achieve this ideal is extremely important."

position—one more task to be done or a burden to be endured—
and energy expenditure will be kept at a minimum. Sometimes
one comes across a community where the liturgy has been dead
for decades, its forms frozen and meaningless, its books tattered,
and its chanting ragged. Absences and late-coming are rampant,
because nobody really wants to be at the liturgy; there are many
alternative occupations that are more useful and more gratifying.
Such a community has lost one of its identifying characteristics,
and it is no surprise that morale is low and recruitment feeble.

Monastic liturgy is typically marked by *gravitas*. Its keynotes
are simplicity and sobriety.[25] It purposely lacks both the fervid
enthusiasm of youth liturgies and the pretentious pomp of pontifical performances. This is because it is expressive of a fundamentally contemplative life and is designed to support and sustain
those attitudes that contribute to an avowedly prayerful existence.
As a community matures, and as the average age of its members
increases, there will also be a noticeable preference for quieter
celebrations in which variety and much-speaking are less important. Like the monks and nuns themselves, the liturgy is unobtru-
sively becoming more apophatic.

b. The monastery as church will take the Gospel as its guide
(RB Prol. 21), understanding that the Scriptures are the most effective norm for human life (RB 73.3). This involves a double
exposure to the Scriptures. The Word of God must be proclaimed
to the community as the necessary soul that complements and
animates the body of observances. Indeed, Saint Benedict man-
dates that the abbot should not teach, establish as policy, or command anything outside what the Lord has enjoined (RB 2.4: *nihil
extra praeceptum Domini*). It is in response to the daily challenge
of Scripture that possibility arises of infusing otherwise banal
actions with authentic spiritual content. The Word of God heard

25. See Michael Casey, "Monasticism and Liturgy," *Tjurunga* 91 (2018):
5–19.

in community needs to be buttressed by personal *lectio divina*—
long considered as the vibrant heart of Benedictine *conversatio*.
For the Gospel to be translated into action there needs also to be
an environment that is conducive to reflection. The words of the
sacred text do not immediately translate into practical directives;
they need to be pondered, ruminated, assimilated.

c. The monastery as church will have at the forefront of its
concerns the spiritual flourishing of each of its members.[26] The
work and prayer of monks and nuns is effective only to the extent
that these activities flow from an undivided heart so that there is
no impedance standing between what they are and what they do.
The purity of heart that the ancient monks sought with so much
zeal permits the action of God to flow through the person, unhin-
dered by self-will, arrogance, or ambition. Monasteries should be
places where people grow spiritually. This demands personalized
pastoral care: the abbot is reminded that his governance should
be at the service of the different characters found in the community
(RB 2.31: *multorum servire moribus*) and not some species of
tyranny (RB 27.6).[27] The visible mission of the community—
whatever that may be—derives from the fact that its members
have been called by God; it is only by cultivating an ongoing
sensitivity to that call that persons and their activities flourish.

In giving emphasis to the spiritual and ecclesial character of
monastic community we hope to provide a prism through which

26. "Because religious community is a *Schola amoris* which helps one grow
in love for God and for one's brothers and sisters, it is also a place for human
growth" (CICLSAL, *Congregavit nos in unum Christi amor [Fraternal Life in
Community]*: [1994], §35).

27. On this see Dysmas de Lassus, *Risques et dérives de la vie religieuse*
(Paris: Cerf, 2020).

we may discuss the more practical aspects of living together in community. It is easy to be overwhelmed by the day-to-day concerns of community life and activity so that the fundamental purpose of pursuing our vocation fades from active view. In any discussion, we need to keep in mind the primary source of our identity as the integrating principle of all we do. This is stated quite clearly in a recent document from the Vatican:

> At the basis of every journey, we find it important to underline the need for consecrated men and women to have a new aspiration for holiness, which is unthinkable without a jolt of renewed passion for the Gospel at the service of the Kingdom. We are moved to this journey by the Spirit of the Risen One who continues to speak to the Church through his inspirations.[28]

Perhaps we need to assess situations and challenges according to a different and distinctive scale of values.

It is the sacred character of the monastic community that is its most distinctive feature. Its role as a visible sign of the church is to witness to the presence of the risen Christ to an indifferent world and to be a sign of hope to a generation that sometimes seems to be fading into despair. By the attractiveness of their fully realized humanity monks and nuns can be lights on a hilltop, trailblazers for all who wish to follow Christ, who is our road to eternal life.

But a word of warning. A monastic community is not Utopia. Every community that I have ever known embraces not only holy and well-integrated people; there is room for a few laggards as well. Every spiritual journey includes stages of regression during which a person's worst features emerge, whether these be psychological, moral, or spiritual. Like the universal Church, we are

---

28. CICLSAL, *New Wine in New Wineskins: The Consecrated Life and its Ongoing Challenges since Vatican II* (2017), §10.

a community of those blighted by sin. This is why Saint Benedict calls upon us to expect to put up with both bodily and moral weaknesses in those around us (RB 72.5). This patience is our principal means of sharing in the paschal mystery (RB Prol. 50). Whatever image our public relations people try to market, the monastic community is always marked with the sign of the cross, willingly embraced as the only path that leads to eternal life.

2

Common Prayer

The Liturgy of the Hours is usually named *Opus Dei* in monastic circles. This is the term used several times in the body of Saint Benedict's Rule, though, curiously, not in the section dealing explicitly with the Office (RB 8–20).[1] The term probably indicates that the choral Office is a "task" more than a "labor." The Liturgy of the Hours is the chief communal activity. Apart from meals, only the Office consistently draws the community together in a single enterprise every day. Monks work wherever there are tasks to be done, *lectio divina* is an individual exercise, and "Each is to sleep in a separate bed" (RB 22.1). It is primarily at the Office, that—at least aspirationally—all together engage in a corporate activity. Perhaps the sociological significance of the Office is as important as its spiritual function. It is the principal structuring element in the monastic day and, probably, the best indicator of the quality of the community's life together. It is an expression of the fundamental identity of the community.

In the wake of the Second Vatican Council liturgists often spoke about "the sanctification of time."[2] As in Judaism and Islam, the

---

1. RB 7.63; 22.6, 8; 43t, 3, 6, 10; 44.1, 7; 47t, 1; 50.3; 52.2, 5; 58.7; 67.2, 3.

2. Vatican II, *Sacrosanctum Concilium* 84, 86, 94; Paul VI, *Sacrificium laudis* (1966) and *Laudis canticum* (1970). See the section on the Liturgy of the Hours

whole day is considered to be consecrated to God by being punctuated by fixed times of prayer. This practice has been in evidence
from the earliest centuries of the church. The theology of the
Office is presented in the 1971 *General Instruction on the Liturgy
of the Hours* (GILH), usually printed in the first volume of the
Breviary.[3] Here our focus will be more on the experiential aspects
of celebrating the Hours in a monastic context.

Sometimes the meaning of the monastic Office is sought in
terms of the much-lauded pursuit of continuous prayer.[4] And so
David Steindl-Rast describes it as a trellis on which a more enduring prayer can grow.[5] Adalbert de Vogüé speaks of the Hours as
the pylons supporting a bridge over which unimpeded traffic between earth and heaven can flow.[6] In such conceptions, continuous
prayer is created from or, at least, facilitated by what we do. Something of the gratuitous and invasive nature of pure prayer is lost.

I have questions about the status of an aspiration to continuous
prayer, even if the achievement of that goal were likely or, indeed,
possible. I think that the most we can aim for is for prayer to

---

under the heading "La Sanctification du temps," in *L'Église en prière: Introduction à la liturgie* (Paris: Desclée, 1965), 809–902. See also Conference of
American Benedictine Prioresses, *Of Time Made Holy: A Statement on the Liturgy
of the Hours in the Lives of American Benedictine Sisters* (Madison, WI, 1978).

3. See also A. M. Roguet, *The Liturgy of the Hours: The General Instruction
on the Liturgy of the Hours with a Commentary* (Sydney, Australia: E. J. Dwyer,
1971). A monastic supplement to this was mandated in 1973, and published as
Directorium de Opere Dei persolvendo in *Thesaurus Liturgiae Horarum Mo-
nasticae* (Rome: Office of the Abbot Primate, 1977), 4–18. In English: Anne M.
Field, ed., *The Monastic Hours: Directory for the Celebration of the Work of
God and Directive Norms for the Celebration of the Monastic Liturgy of the
Hours,* 2nd ed. (Collegeville, MN: Liturgical Press, 2000).

4. It seems to me that *continuous* or unbroken prayer is possible only in
heaven; while we are on earth the most that we can hope for is *continual*, or
stop-and-start prayer.

5. David Steindl-Rast, *The Music of Silence* (San Francisco: Harper, 1995), 9.

6. Adalbert de Vogüé, "Prayer in the Rule of St Benedict," *Monastic Studies*
7 (1969): 113–40.

become a default state, something to which we slip back when nothing else demands our attention, like a pendulum coming to rest at its lowest point. I am reminded of the dangers portrayed in J. D. Salinger's *Franny and Zooey*.[7] In such a situation prayer seems to be becoming a tyranny, trying to displace all that is not explicit prayer. Is there no value in anything else? Am I to understand that sleeping, eating mindfully, engaging in heartfelt conversation, and concentrating on complex tasks are all of lesser importance and should scarcely merit my concern? As Sir Toby Belch exclaims in Shakespeare's *Twelfth Night,* "Dost thou think because thou art virtuous, there shall be no more cakes and ale?"[8] Saint Jerome seems to have been of a similar opinion:

> The human mind is not able always to stretch out to the sublime and to think about divine and loftier matters, nor is it able to be permanently in contemplation of heavenly realities. Sometimes it must defer to bodily necessities. There is a time for embracing wisdom and for clinging to it more closely, and a time for relaxing the mind from the gaze and embrace of wisdom so that it might be of service to the care of the body and to those things that are needed for our life— apart from sin.[9]

7. J. D. Salinger, *Franny and Zooey* (Harmondsworth: Penguin Books, 1975).

8. Act 2, Scene 3.

9. Saint Jerome, *Commentarius in Ecclesiasten*, PL 23:1089C. See also the *Glossa ordinaria* on Eccl 3:5: *Et propter corpoream necessitatem, tempus est relaxandi mentem a complexu sapientiae, ut curae corporis serviatur:* "Because of bodily necessity, there is a time for relaxing the mind from the embrace of wisdom, so that care of the body may be maintained" (Jennifer Lynn Kostoff-Käärd, "The 'Glossa Ordinaria' on Ecclesiastes: A Critical Edition with Introduction," PhD Thesis from the Centre for Mediaeval Studies, University of Toronto, 2015, 206). See also Pope Paul VI, *Apostolic Exhortation on Christian Joy* (May 9, 1975): "There is also needed a patient effort to teach people, or teach them once more, how to savour in a simple way the many human joys that the Creator places in our path."

On one occasion a monk driving me to the airport suggested my reading the Breviary aloud, so as "to get the Office done." He was disedified when I demurred, saying that I would much rather look out the window, since it was unlikely that I would ever pass that way again. To my mind, God deserves more than multitasking. Likewise, a confrere who as a layman was chauffeuring Father Peyton, the Family Rosary Crusader, expressed himself disappointed that he did not have the opportunity to ask advice, because the zealous priest kept saying the rosary aloud for the entire journey. In a similar situation, during the Council, Cardinal Ottaviani and his arch-foe Karl Rahner were both attending a conference. The cardinal invited the theologian to travel with him, and the latter thought it would offer an occasion for dialogue. But no. The cardinal preempted that possibility by multiple rosaries.

It seems to me that theories about monastic life as the pursuit of continuous prayer may fail to respect the inherent dignity and humanity of other necessary or useful activities. This is especially so when prayer is viewed as a sequence of actions to be done rather than as a state into which one is subtly drawn. There is inherent spiritual meaning in every human good; spirituality does not have to be superimposed, as it were, from outside or from above. The ordinary, obscure, and laborious activities of daily life, particularly those that are recommended in the Gospel, are not enemies of prayer. Oddly enough, these everyday occupations are probably the most potent determinants of the quality of explicit prayer, as John Cassian notes: "Whatever we wish to be found when we pray, we have to prepare before the time of prayer. From its previous condition, the mind at prayer is formed."[10]

Today the principal daily occupation of a typical Cistercian monk is sleeping. This consumes seven to eight hours. Then follows work, for four to six hours. Liturgy may take about three to four hours and personal prayer and reading another two or three hours. He spends an hour or so eating, and the remaining few hours

10. John Cassian, *Conferences* 9.3; SCh 54:42.

are filled with personal activities and with community interactions. Each of these activities plays a role in assuring the integrity of monastic life; none may be arbitrarily left aside. It is the whole complex of different activities that is life-giving. Harmony is broken when one activity is expanded at the expense of others so that inner discord results, eventually with visible consequences.

I see the specific value of the Liturgy of the Hours as interruption. The practice introduces into our lives the grace of discontinuity. We stop whatever we are doing and turn our attention to something different. This opens up gaps in our everyday living during which we are not totally engaged with whatever it is that totally engages us. When monks lived in a world without clocks, determining the time for the Office was an important task (RB 47.1). The monks were often caught out by a sudden summons. Yet they were expected to drop whatever was in their hands and "run very quickly but with gravity" to arrive punctually at the oratory (RB 43.1-2). In the morning, likewise, they had to hasten with gravity, vying with one another, to be first to assemble (RB 22.6). It is this combination of haste and gravity that I find interesting. Zeal for the *Opus Dei* is recommended, but it must be combined with *gravitas*, so that a mental space may be created between the previous occupation and community prayer. Participation in the Hour begins when the monk sets aside whatever he is doing, when he puts the computer to sleep and stands up, ready to move off. Already he is creating a receptive space for whatever the liturgy offers. Arriving late or out of breath is reprehensible not merely because it can be a sign of willful disorganization or passive aggression, but also because it means arriving at the Office in a state of mental, and probably spiritual, upheaval. The various moments leading up to the beginning of the Hour serve as preparation for integral participation in the liturgy:

> The transition from a certain dispersion (a diversity of duties and engagements and consequently of mental preoccupations) to that unity which the celebration presupposes (and brings about) can only be made if the mind deliberately and

consciously relinquishes such multiplicity in order to prepare for a unity which is before all else interior.[11]

The style of movement demanded by the traditional cloister
and the practice of *statio* contribute to a state of disengagement
preliminary to prayer. It is a practical recognition that the *Opus
Dei* is something quite distinct from other activities and that
monks need a few moments to change the focus of their thoughts.
Certainly, it involves a physical pause, slowing down the heart
rate and the breathing. Perhaps also mentally switching from the
left-hemisphere activity to the right. On the other hand, running
to arrive in the nick of time will almost certainly mean the undermining of attention as the liturgy unfolds. Any observer of body
language can easily verify this.

The Liturgy of the Hours is an invitation to come away to the
desert so that God may speak to the heart. It involves leaving
behind the world of practical utility, allowing tasks to be left
undone or unfinished in order to stand before God. If you were to
ask monks or nuns on their way to the Office what they expected
to receive from it most would be left speechless. In part, going to
the Office is routine, but it is more than that. It is yielding control—moving from a zone of activity into a condition of respon-
siveness and service. There is no explicit agenda in going to the
Office except being there and allowing the liturgy to work its
magic on us. We are open to being moved. "As the eyes of servants
are on the hands of their masters, or the eyes of handmaids on the
hands of their mistresses," so we stand in attendance before God
awaiting direction, not neglecting to render to God the burden of
our service (RB 50.4).

The Office begins by recognizing the transition. Vigils begins
with a wake-up verse ("O Lord, open my lips"). This is followed
by the Invitatory psalm. The other Hours begin with the verse, "O

---

11. Field, *The Monastic Hours*, 36, §18.

God, come to my assistance."[12] This is in accordance with the injunction in the Rule's Prologue: "As you begin doing anything good, ask with most pressing prayer that it will be brought to completion by [Christ]." We perceive the challenge of transitioning into prayer, and we ask for God's help in meeting it, affirming thereby that the grace of prayer is God's gift.

Every Office is composed of several different elements: psalms, a hymn, a reading, and a prayer, plus other minor components. Together they constitute an invitation for the monk or nun to enter a different space in which they may freely give expression to what is most important to them and then hear a response. It has been wisely suggested that the celebration of the Hours should incorporate both recurring and changeable elements, so that familiarity does not breed contempt and novelty does not hijack most of the attention.[13]

Hymns, Psalms, Readings, and Prayers: each of these essential elements has an important and distinctive role to play in the liturgical celebration.

Hymns: Despite some of Saint Benedict's arrangements, hymns work best as "an easy and pleasant opening to the prayer" (GILH §42). Heartfelt singing together often has the effect of transforming a crowd into a community, as can be seen at British football matches. Finding hymns with which a community may fully identify is not always easy. Good hymnody must combine solid content, poetic expression, good music, and suitability to the particular group. Accordingly, some think that hymns should never be translated and that they must always be sung—never merely recited. There are many challenges in finding suitable

---

12. No doubt the choice of this verse was influenced by John Cassian's celebration of its universal relevance (*Conferences* 10.10; SCh 54:85–90).

13. "In ordering the celebration of the Liturgy of the Hours a balance is maintained between the recurrence of familiar elements and the introduction of new ones, so that the celebration reassures by repetition and refreshes by surprise" (*Of Time Made Holy*, §34).

hymns. Sometimes the music is too difficult. Sometimes English does not suit cherished Gregorian melodies. Sometimes the text is too dense or esoteric. Sometimes the hymns belong to a cultural ambience alien to the community.[14] Finding or composing new hymns is an ongoing task.

Psalms: Vocalization of the psalms has the effect of making it difficult to think about anything else, and so it becomes a means of pushing potential distractions from the mind.[15] This advantage vanishes when the psalms become so familiar that their recitation demands little by way of attention. In this situation, monks and nuns can be doing no more than opening and closing their mouths like goldfish in a bowl, while their thoughts are a thousand miles away. More optimistically, when familiarity wears down the rational edge of the text, the psalm can become transparent, serving to connect the singer's devotion with God in a consciously I-Thou relationship. More ordinarily, however, the psalms provide grist for the mill of meditation, evoking a variety of responses ranging from dread-filled despair to warm thanksgiving and jubilant praise. This is because the psalms are poetry—their primary appeal is to the intuitive right side of our brain, and so they are able to provide a medium for the expression of the deepest feelings of our hearts: "Whoever sings a psalm opens his heart to those emotions which inspired the psalm, each according to its literary type" (GILH §106). The psalms are a primary formative influence on the spirituality of monks and nuns, as can be seen by the frequency with which they are cited by monastic writers. A lifetime of singing the psalms is a potent agent in spiritual literacy; it provides a language by which even the most esoteric interior states can be grasped and expressed.

14. For a survey of hymnody in different regions see the whole issue of *La Maison-Dieu* 151 (1982): "Chanter Dieu: Chanter pour Dieu."

15. On the other hand, it has been my experience that when I participate in the Office in a foreign language I have to concentrate so much more on getting the words of the unfamiliar text in the right sequence that their meaning often escapes me, and, furthermore, any deeper resonances become increasingly rare.

Readings: Apart from Vigils, the readings of the Office frequently receive scant attention. They are mostly short and frequently repeated—indeed Saint Benedict envisages lessons being recited by heart (RB 9.10; 10.2; 12.4; 13.11). If the community oversleeps, the lessons may be shortened (RB 11.12). In such cases, the reader rattles through the text while the community impatiently waits for it to finish. Is this the kind of attention that the Word of God merits? On the other hand, it has to be said also that the longer readings at Vigils do not always provide nourishment for prayer. Saint Benedict's injunction in another context about avoiding the more graphic narratives of the Old Testament could well be heeded. Not many monks and nuns find unction in hearing about the Maccabees slaughtering unbelievers, so mostly they switch off. It is scarcely worth getting out of bed to listen to such narratives. Reading even a brief lesson needs to be surrounded by a mild degree of solemnity: a brief pause while the community sits down to listen, and a careful reading by one who is competent to read well and earnest enough to bring edification to the listeners (RB 38.12).

Prayer: Of course, the whole Office may be understood as prayer in a general sense, but it is usual for the multiple strands of the office to be collected in a concluding prayer. Perhaps reflecting the practice mentioned in the *Didache*,[16] Saint Benedict includes the Lord's Prayer at each of the Offices but with more solemnity at Lauds and Vespers (RB 13.12-14). In addition, there is the possibility of a few moments of silent prayer, but "care should be taken that such a silence neither deforms the structure of the Office, nor upsets or bores the participants" (GILH §202).

These primary elements are supplemented by other features such as antiphons and responsories, according to the possibilities enjoyed by each community. Intercessions are meant to be petitionary; too often they are faintly disguised moralizing, in which we pray that others will upgrade their behavior. In all this, the

---

16. *Didache* 8.3; Bart D. Ehrman, ed., *The Apostolic Fathers*, vol. 1 (Cambridge: Harvard University Press, 2005), 430.

main concern must be that the liturgy both expresses and contributes to the unity of the community. Not infrequently the liturgy
is one of the main areas of contention in a community, with the
bulk of the community pitted against the professional musicians,
and those with high-church tastes arm-wrestling with the liturgical
minimalists. This is a situation that needs to be addressed, even
if the conflict rises to the surface only rarely. Participation must
always be given priority over performance. It may be nice to have
a liturgy that plays well on television, but it is more important that
those taking part find in it a medium of prayer.

The importance of the liturgy in the Rule of Saint Benedict is
obvious from the many chapters devoted to it and from the frequency with which he references it in dealing with other matters.
There are eight principles enunciated in the Rule that suggest
attitudes appropriate to our participation in the liturgy.[17] May I be
forgiven for recalling what is probably obvious to all who have
lived the monastic life for any length of time.

The first principle involves acceptance of the burden of obligation, the *servitutis pensum* (RB 50.4 and 16.2). The Liturgy of
the Hours is not something in which we participate when we feel
so inclined; it is an ongoing task that we have freely embraced in
making profession. Sometimes it takes an effort to drag ourselves
away from some creative and necessary task to join the communal
drone in the church; we do so only because we have to. And it is
not merely a duty to attend choir; the obligation follows us around
whether we are working in the fields or abroad on an important
journey (RB 50). We are not canons responsible to see that the
church's liturgy is duly performed; somehow the obligation clings
more tightly to us because of what we are. This is not to say that
we must become scrupulous, but it is a firm reminder that we do
not allow ourselves to become lackadaisical about the Office, or
flippantly ready to dispense ourselves from it on the slightest
pretext.

17. See Michael Casey, "The Discipline of Psalmody: RB 19," *Tjurunga* 68
(2005): 57–79.

A second principle is the often-quoted axiom: "Nothing is to be given priority over the Work of God" (RB 43.3). It sounds like, and is often quoted as, an absolute principle, but, in context, it refers simply to the work in which a monk is engaged when the signal for the Office sounds. If someone collapses in the cloister with a heart attack it is not necessary to wait until the liturgy is over before giving assistance. What Saint Benedict means is that the Office is of such high importance that activities of less importance, as well as imagined urgencies, should not displace it. This is stated not only as an organizational principle, but also as something to be internalized by each monk and nun. The Liturgy of the Hours is to be embraced as the foundation of daily life. It plays a dynamic role in spiritual development.

So it is not surprising that, as a third principle, Saint Benedict sees solicitude with regard to the Work of God as one of the indicators of a genuine vocation (RB 58.7). This is more than an interest in liturgy. It indicates a capacity to find prayer in the Liturgy of the Hours, so that it becomes a source of devotion and, thereby, a means by which the *dura et aspera* of monastic life can be endured. If the Office is mere ceremonial or if it is borne as a meaningless obligation, it will not have the power to equip the novice to face the challenges that transitioning into monastic life brings. Out of sweetness comes strength.

The fourth principle is "Serve the Lord in fear" (RB 19.3). This is a quotation of Psalm 2:11. The second half of the verse is, "And trembling pay him your homage." This suggests the idea of vassals rendering due homage to their lord and emphasizes the idea of duty rather than of spontaneity. It is performed seriously and with respect—not as something that we can manipulate to suit ourselves.

Unsurprisingly, the fifth principle enunciates the subjective conditions under which this worship is to be offered: "With humility and reverence" (RB 20.1). To act otherwise is to be guilty of presumption. The remainder of chapter 20 spells out the details. God must be approached in the Office or at other times not with a profusion of meaningless words but with sincere devotion. The texts of the Office matter only in so far as they provoke an echoing response in the heart.

Such reverence will more likely be inspired by arriving at the Office with a strong sense of entering sacred space. Here monastic custom provides an external vehicle for such reverence: the wearing of the cowl, *gravitas*, profound bows. If we had before our minds the image of joining the angels in the heavenly court, I imagine we would be less flippant in our approach. The *Exordium Magnum* tells of a vision in which a monk saw the choir of Cîteaux with the angels forming a second choir above the heads of the monks, bowing in unison with them.[18] Though fanciful, the story underlines the significance of Saint Benedict's sixth principle, that we sing, conscious of the presence of the angels (RB 19.5). As Pope John-Paul II wrote somewhat optimistically, "The liturgy is heaven on earth."[19]

The seventh principle is the injunction to sing psalms wisely, as the quoted text enjoins (RB 19.4; Ps 138:1).[20] Objectively this text could refer to the quality of the music, that what is chosen is suitable for worship but also appropriate for the community that makes use of it. Subjectively it may be suggesting that a certain amount of work should be undertaken to appreciate the different levels of meaning to be found in the scriptural text. This probably presupposes a study of the psalms outside the time of liturgy (RB 8.3).[21] Saint Augustine reminds us that

> Blackbirds, parrots, crows, magpies and other such birds may be taught to make the sound of words they do not understand, but by God's will it has been given to human nature to sing knowingly. . . . What we have sung with harmoni-

18. *Exordium Magnum,* Dist. I, Cap. 34 (Rome: Editiones Cistercienses, 1961), 94–95.

19. John-Paul II, *Orientale lumen* §11.

20. See Don Simone Barbieri, "Cantate con arte, o sorelle," *Vita Nostra* 19 (2020): 82–91.

21. Michael Casey, "The Prayer of Psalmody," CSQ 18, no. 2 (1983): 106–20.

ous voice we ought also to know and see with a tranquil heart.[22]

The final principle, probably borrowed from Saint Augustine, is that the mind should be in harmony with the voice (RB 19.7). This theme is one that many authors discuss with great enthusiasm. We are called to understand what we sing, but for this to happen we have to pay attention. Paying attention means more than liberating ourselves from our intrusive or obsessive daily preoccupations; it means a conscious effort to concentrate on the text, bringing to it all the interior resources of mind and heart that we have allowed to develop over the years.

In line with their reformist agenda, the early Cistercians placed more emphasis on intelligent participation than on the splendor of liturgical celebration.[23] Their chief concern was to upgrade the quality of attention with which the liturgy was executed. This involved confronting the reality of distraction. John of Forde (d. 1214) noted that distractions deprive us of the spiritual uplift that the Office can give and so make the liturgy more onerous—something to be endured rather than enjoyed. He distinguished four species of distraction:

> If you think about it, there are in fact four kinds of thoughts that are, of course, always a nuisance, but that are at their most troublesome and importunate at the very time when we take part in the Divine Office.
> The first is more dangerous than the others, determined to stain our mind, or rather, to infect it with its poison of

---

22. Augustine, *On Psalm 18*, 2.1; SCh 38:105.

23. It was found necessary to offer a catechesis on the meaning of the traditional hymns, *quia non intelligebant obscuritatem verborum legendo sive canendo, minor eorum devotio habebatur.* Thus the treatise, *Explanatio super hymnos quibus utitur Ordo Cisterciensis* §1, ed. John Michael Beers (Gainsborough: Henry Bradshaw Society, 1982), 1. The treatise was probably written in the final quadrant of the twelfth century.

physical lust or some kind of non-physical passion, such as pride, ambition, envy, or anger.

But the second kind is of vain and empty thoughts, the sort with which we are slackly accustomed to waste the time set apart for penance by chatting and retailing vulgarities. We do not want them at our prayers and in choir, but we deserve to have the burden of them, since we have willingly and knowingly given them entrance.

The third kind of temptation is to thoughts of our daily lives, when the things we are anxious about are accustomed to preoccupy us. These lead us all the more subtly astray in that they disguise themselves under the pretext of serving our own or the common good.

Last, there is the fourth kind of temptation, which covers itself with what one might call the outer appearance of innocence, yes, and even of sanctity. There will come into our memory, for instance, something from our yesterday's reading or some other passages of holy Scripture, displacing what is actually before us, and because of these thoughts, we fast from what has been set out for us to eat.[24]

So important is our concentration on the text before us that John advises us to set aside any other kind of holy thought in order to concentrate on what we are singing. Similar views are expressed by Bernard of Clairvaux:

I say that psalmody should be performed with a pure heart to indicate that, during psalmody, you should not be thinking of anything except the Psalm itself. Nor do I mean that only vain and useless thoughts are to be avoided. At that time and in that place are to be avoided those necessary thoughts about necessary community matters that frequently importune the minds of those brothers who have official positions. Further-

24. John of Forde, *Sermons on the Song of Songs* 87.8, trans. Wendy Mary Beckett, CF 46 (Kalamazoo, MI: Cistercian Publications, 1984), 56–57; CCCM 18:597.

more, my advice is that even those thoughts are to be left aside that come from attending on the Holy Spirit before psalmody begins, for example, as you sit in the cloister or read books or as you listen to my conference, as you do now. These are wholesome thoughts, but it is not at all wholesome to reflect upon them during psalmody. At such a time the Holy Spirit is not pleased to receive what you offer apart from what you owe, since you are neglecting to render your due.[25]

Another twelfth-century Cistercian, Arnulph of Bohéries (ca. 1175), makes an exception to this rule in the case of ecstatic transports—no doubt a relief for the average monk or nun:

During psalmody one should give one's whole attention to the Psalms; the only exception is one's being caught away to something more sublime. Yes, one should be attentive to all that is said during the Office, knowing for sure that one will have to answer for every last letter of every word, either uttering it on one's own side of choir or listening to it from the other.[26]

This emphasis on the verbal content of chant meant that priority was to be given to the verbal content; the music should serve the meaning and not distract from it. Saint Bernard makes this point in a letter to the Victorine Abbot Guy of Montier-Ramey:

The sense of the words should be unmistakable, and they should shine with truth, tell of righteousness, incite to humility, and inculcate justice; they should bring truth to the minds of the hearers, devotion to their affections, the cross to their vices, and discipline to their senses. If there is to be singing, the melody should be grave and not flippant or uncouth. It

25. Bernard of Clairvaux, SC 47.8; SBOp 2:66.
26. "The Monk's Mirror," trans. Hugh McCaffrey, OCSO, *Tjurunga* 55 (1998): 35–36.

should be sweet but not frivolous, it should both enchant the
ears and move the heart, it should lighten sad hearts and
soften angry passions, it should never obscure but enhance
the sense of the words. Not a little spiritual profit is lost
when minds are distracted from the sense of the words by
the frivolity of the melody, when more is conveyed by the
modulations of the voice than by variations of meaning.[27]

Bernard envisaged monastic chant as vigorous and, at least for
men, manly. He wanted his monks to put their hearts into the
chant, so that they would sing strenuously:

> Strenuously so that just as you serve the Lord reverently, so
> you would do so enthusiastically, not lazily or sleepily, not
> yawning, not sparing your voices, not cutting the words in
> half or jumping over whole words, not with restrained little
> voices like women, not stammering or singing through the
> nose but, as is only right, in a manly way in both sound and
> in feeling, proclaiming the words of the Holy Spirit.[28]

The exhortation to undeviating concentration on the words
being used is easily made but probably unrealistic to put into
practice all the time. This was particularly so in the Middle Ages,
when mostly the psalms were recited from memory and books
were used sparingly. It is a little easier for us, since we can anchor
our eyes to the text in front of us and our mental energies do not
have to be divided between remembering the words and simultaneously processing them. Even so, it may be possible to achieve
some fusion of horizons when a text is chanted slowly with space
for dialogical reflection, or in the time of resting between verses
in antiphonal chanting. But this kind of interior conversation is
very challenging when a psalm keeps surging forward, sometimes

27. Bernard of Clairvaux, Ep 398.2; SBOp 8:378:9–16.
28. Bernard of Clairvaux, SC 47.8; SBOp 2:66.

rapidly switching purviews and leaving us stranded on the previous verse. The most we can hope for is that *sometimes* the psalm will become for us a kind of a mirror in which the movements of our inner self can be glimpsed. Alas, too often we will be in a kind of daze, with nothing exciting our attention beyond the familiar forward movement of the words.

There is a dynamic operative in psalmody similar to that which operates in our reading of Scripture. The words of the text may well yield a meaning that is fuller than a first perusal many suggest. We may well encounter the four senses of Scripture in our daily psalmody. Sometimes we simply glide along with the literal sense of the text, conscious of its clear meaning. This happens especially with psalms that have a historical character or with those of descriptive praise. In royal psalms and those invested with messianic significance we may move to the allegorical sense, finding poetic expressions that refer to the mystery of Christ. Sometimes, for example in the seemingly repetitive verses of Psalm 119, we may hear a message for our own life, a challenge or invitation to conversion. And often, in all sorts of psalms but especially in the laments, we may find a trigger of prayer that rises up unbidden as we give ourselves to chanting. In these varied ways—perhaps only after years of practice—we may discover that the daily Office can become for us a source of heartfelt prayer. And when other occupations devour our energies, it becomes a relief to participate in the Office and have the opportunity to find ourselves again.

The Office is meant to be something to which monks and nuns give themselves fully, setting aside every other useful occupation and preoccupation and opening their hearts to the grace of the moment. A lifelong dedication to wholehearted participation in the Liturgy of the Hours, buttressed by *lectio divina* and personal prayer, will, almost certainly, bring about a progressive transformation in the person's consciousness and attitudes, and the slow evangelizing of daily life.

3

Hearers of the Word

The title of this chapter is adapted from a book by Karl Rahner first published in 1941 and revised and republished by Johannes Metz in 1963.[1] Its basic thesis is that we attain our full humanity only to the extent that we are open to the Word, God's self-revelation. Since the church and the community may be considered as the place *par excellence* in which we can hear and listen to this Word, attention to the Word, both as a community and as persons, must be considered a prime element of monastic observance. Devotion to the Word is the most powerful driver of both individual and corporate growth. When members of a community live responsive to the Word, harmony results.

In the early 1960s, a prospective candidate for monastic life in a distant part of Australia asked for some information. By chance someone familiar with our monastery was traveling to that region, and we asked him to hand-carry the relevant literature so that he could explain anything that was unclear. And so, he met the aspirant. When asked the meaning of the term *lectio divina* which appeared on the daily schedule, he replied. "Oh, that's when the monks wash and shave, and do things like that."

1. Karl Rahner, *Hearers of the Word*, trans. Michael Richards (New York: Herder and Herder, 1969).

I published my first article on *lectio divina* in 1976, and in 1995 I wrote what I believed was the first complete book devoted to the topic—at least in English.[2] From those times in which the term was generally unfamiliar outside monastic circles, it has gradually entered into the commonplace discourse of Christian spirituality. Notwithstanding this, the 1992 *Catechism of the Catholic Church* has only two sentences in which the term occurs.[3] A rapid reading of a selection of documents from Vatican sources reveals a fairly tepid level of support for *lectio divina*, although it becomes warmer with the passage of time, until the 2008 Synod of Bishops was dedicated to the topic—*The Word of God in the Life and Mission of the Church*—and in 2010 Pope Benedict XVI recapitulated the discussions in his apostolic exhortation *Verbum Domini*.[4]

On July 6, 2020, a Google search for "*lectio divina*" yielded some 7,680,000 hits. This seems to indicate that the term has passed far beyond the confines of the monastic world and even of Catholicism. With this broader usage comes the possibility that the term itself has become inflated to include all sorts of practices not originally signified. It seems that any kind of vaguely reflective reading of the Scriptures can come under the heading of *lectio divina*. It is applied to short inspirational quotations meant to provide a thought for the day, as well as to long exegetical commentaries on liturgical texts, meant to serve as the basis of homilies. We have to conclude that some of this looseness may have crept into monastic consciousness, so that even though we continue to use the traditional term *lectio divina*, its meaning may

2. Michael Casey, "Seven Principles of *Lectio Divina*," *Tjurunga* 12 (1976): 69–74; *The Art of Sacred Reading* (North Blackburn, Australia: Dove, 1995). Subsequently republished as *Sacred Reading: The Ancient Art of Lectio Divina* (Liguori, MO: Triumph Books, 1996). Note that the book of García M. Colombás had long preceded it: *La lectura de Dios: Approximación a la lectio divina* (Zamora, Spain: Ediciones Monte Casino, 1980).

3. §1177 and §2708.

4. *Verbum Domini* §86–87.

have drifted away from what is most helpful for those pursuing a monastic life.

And so it seems worthwhile to try to formulate a description of this quintessential monastic practice, not merely for the sake of technical precision, but also as a guide to everyday practice.

Again, good theory will lead us to good practice. To someone peeping through the window of a monastic cell while a monk or nun is engaged in *lectio divina*, it may seem that they are simply reading a book—it could be a novel or a cookery book or a history of art in Western Europe. Or it could be the Bible studied with a view to completing an assignment in Biblical Studies. Objectively speaking, *lectio divina* seems similar to ordinary reading. The difference is to be found in the reader's subjective attitude to the text. The text is approached with reverence, in a spirit of anteced- ent willingness to hear and to obey. This obedience, however, is given not so much to the material content of the text as to the echo caused by the text in the heart and conscience of the reader. The message embedded in the text passes into daily life only through the medium of the reader's subjective disposition; it is filtered through conscience. Two persons hearing or reading the same text can be triggered differently, depending on their life situations at the time of encounter.

Lectio divina is not intended simply as an exercise to give monks and nuns something to do to keep them out of mischief, nor is it aimed at providing them with some mildly pious entertainment. It is not meant as a source of moral or theological information—or even formation. The primary purpose of *lectio divina* is to actualize—or re-activate—their relationship with God. It re-connects the pipeline to the spiritual world through which energy flows to sustain the person to live a life according to God and, thus, to make a unique contribution to the spiritual heart of the community. It is regular *lectio divina* that preserves the reader from that most wicked vice mentioned only in Col 2:23: *ethelo-* *threskia*—self-made religion—not unknown in contemporary Western society. Real religion is always a response; it is never some complex of beliefs and values concocted by individuals for themselves.

The biblical text, along with some of the more meditative texts of tradition, is the fruit of God's self-revelation. God is chiefly made known through great and kindly interventions in human history—creation, salvation, culmination. The inspired record of these interventions is a means of preserving the memory of the *mirabilia Dei*—the wonderful things God has done—so that those who ponder the written words can spiritually make contact with the inexpressible reality that is somehow conveyed by them. This is done in such a way that the written text becomes for us a *torah*— a source of instruction on how to live.

When we give ourselves to *lectio divina*, we encounter a Thou. We have become so accustomed to this that it no longer surprises us, even though it is truly remarkable. The psalms are not only hymns of descriptive praise about a third-person deity. Many of them invite us to address God directly from whatever situation we find ourselves in, be it ever so dire. And Jesus takes the matter beyond that; as members of God's household, we are to address God by his intra-familial title: *Abba*.

Through the muffled and imperfect words on the page, God is speaking to our hearts, just as has been done in different ages through the patriarchs and the prophets. It is worthwhile remembering that the Holy Spirit is active not only in the composition of the sacred texts but also in their reception. Each of us is called to hear what the Spirit has to say to the churches and to us. Our response must be in the hallowed words of the boy prophet Samuel: "Speak, Lord, for your servant is listening."

An I-Thou approach to *lectio divina* means that we search within the text for what is beyond and behind the written words. Progress in moving forward is slowed because of the need for close reading and rereading, and also for reflection on what has been read. When the fuller sense of the text begins to become apparent it often stirs the heart in a way that generates spontaneous prayer in the region where text and life-experience overlap. *Lectio divina* is punctuated by prayer, not because it is forced, but because it rises naturally when the meaning of the text begins to penetrate. Just as after a cold swim the body is warmed naturally by the rays of the summer sun, so our inmost being becomes sensitive to the intimate presence of God and cannot but respond to it.

This is more than simply reading a book.

If we turn to the Rule of Saint Benedict, the chapter on work provides us with a starting point. In it, Benedict notes that the monastic day (apart from the time spent in liturgy and in attending to various biological necessities) is to be divided between manual work and *lectio divina* (RB 48). The relative proportion of time given to each will vary from season to season and according to the urgency of practical tasks needing attention. To our modern dismay it seems that Saint Benedict anticipated that his monks would spend several hours each day pondering the Scriptures. We ask ourselves where have all the hours gone. We often find it hard enough to create a daily slot in which we "do" our *lectio*. Saint Benedict seems to have a different approach. He seems to regard *lectio divina* as a kind of default practice to which we spontaneously return when nothing else demands our engagement—though, I imagine, he had enough common sense to realize that this was more likely to be true later in the monk's life rather than at the beginning. He recognized that there are monks and nuns unable to spend the extra time on Sunday in reading (RB 48.22-23). To such as these he assigned whatever tasks are necessary to keep the monastery ticking. His other intention in making this provision was to exclude the possibility of acedia, purposeless time-wasting.

It is the considerable length of time spent mulling over the Scriptures that enables monks and nuns to live a life that concords with the Word of God. This is why a monastic community is not merely a gathering of individuals concerned with spiritual advancement but an expression of the ecclesial mystery. The admonition that Benedict wanted proclaimed daily at the start of the Office of Vigils sets the tone for the whole community every day: "If today you hear God's voice, harden not your heart." We who endeavor to live our lives under the guidance of the Gospel are clearly bound to do more than glance at the sacred text from time to time. We are meant to be so permeated by the words and spirit of the Gospel that our actions are stamped with its character. A music critic cannot help feeling uncomfortable when the members of the congregation murder the hymn they are singing. A professional writer or editor cannot help noticing the infelicities of style and the misprints in any book they are reading. A chef cannot help knowing that a meal has been overcooked.[5] So it is to be expected that those who profess to live by the Gospel are perfectly aware of what is in harmony with the life and teaching of Jesus and what contradicts it. At least they will be, if their contact with the Word of God has been sustained over many years and decades.

Before we become too fanatical, it is good to remind ourselves of the importance of prudence. We today probably recognize the importance of necessary periods of rest, recuperation, recreation, and relaxation. We banish such intervals from our lives at our peril. People who try to cram too much into the day inevitably become discouraged or burn out. These unlegislated moments are an important component of Benedictine moderation.[6] The ancient Cistercian customary makes provision for monks simply sitting quietly in the cloister, having a pause between activities. We need to take seriously Saint Benedict's use of the cautionary classical

---

5. This phenomenon is sometimes termed *déformation professionelle*.

6. See Michael Casey, "Moderation: The Key to Permanence," in Gervase Holdawa, ed., *The Oblate Life* (Collegeville, MN: Liturgical Press, 2008), 177–86; " 'Balance' in Monastic Life," *Tjurunga* 9 (1975): 5–11; and "The Benedictine Balances," in *Saint Benedict of Nursia: A Way of Wisdom for Today* (Paris: Editions du Signe, 1994), 24–25. But we also need to heed the cautionary note sounded by David Malouf in *A First Place* (North Sydney, Australia: Knopf, 2014), 301: "the preference for moderation easily leads to mediocrity."

formula, *ne quid nimis*: "not too much" (RB 64.12). It would be wrong to turn monastic life into a joyless state of overregulation or a situation of being tyrannized by the superego or forced into compulsive virtue by a psychological disorder. Wholesome monasteries place a high premium on safeguarding leisure.[7] Pope Francis has frequently spoken of the danger of efficiency squeezing out human values: "Have the courage to go against the tide of this culture of efficiency, this culture of waste."[8]

I think it is probably true to say that we do not, for the most part, leave aside *lectio divina* for the sake of willfully wasting time. Mostly work—whether this be a matter of assigned charges or tasks or self-imposed activities—comes along to push aside everything in its path. From time to time it is useful to see how the hours seem to disappear from the days, the days from the weeks, and the weeks from the years. Not a few people who have the good fortune to arrive at an advanced age often say to themselves or to others, "Where have all the years gone?" We have the words of Jesus to admonish us: "the night is coming when no one can work" (John 9:4). If we want to be serious about our spiritual life, now is the best time to make a start.

The difficulty of calculating how much time we should give to *lectio* every day is compounded by the fact that at different seasons of our life we need a different injection of *lectio* and *lectio*-related activities. Especially in times of transition we are well advised to

7. See Jean Leclercq, *Otia Monastica: Études sur le vocabulaire de la contemplation au Moyen Âge* (Rome: Herder, 1963). See also Michael Casey, "Leisure," in *Strangers to the City: Reflections on the Beliefs and Values of the Rule of Saint Benedict* (Brewster, MA: Paraclete, 2005), 26–37; and "The Grace of Leisure," in *Grace on the Journey to God* (Brewster, MA: Paraclete, 2018), 147–59.

8. Pope Francis, "Homily at XXVIII World Youth Day: 27 July 2013," in *L'Osservatore Romano*, 29–30 July 2013, 4. In an address to the Pontifical Academy of the Social Sciences on 20 October 2017, he said, "We cannot sacrifice on the altar of efficiency—the 'golden calf' of our times—fundamental values such as democracy, justice, freedom, the family, and creation."

step back from some of the activities that fill the hours, and pause to consider our options and to seek the guidance of God in prayer. This is where any attempt at a mechanical computation of the time we need to devote to *lectio* lets us down. Furthermore, at different seasons the proportion of *lectio* considered as time spent with the Bible open before us varies relative to time spent in silent prayer or in personal reflection. As we grow older and perhaps more mature spiritually, we may well be drawn to spend more time in silent prayer, with our daily appetite for God's word adequately satisfied by relatively short exposure.

In general, however, we will probably find it helpful to aim at having a regular time and place for *lectio*. That is, mostly, how we live our lives. We fit more into every day by crafting a sequence of activities that either flow into one another or, alternatively, provide a change of rhythm that is energizing. This reduces the number of decisions we make in the course of the day—and eliminates the time spent in weighing our options—and, perhaps, thereby exposes us to the temptation of using the available time for other pursuits. Regularity does not necessarily imply rigidity. Just as buildings that are somewhat flexible cope better with earthquakes, so the most effective means of incorporating *lectio divina* into our daily schedule is one that understands that to every rule there are necessary exceptions.

We should not be afraid to experiment with what we do during our time of *lectio*. Not only with times and places but also how we conduct ourselves as we read. Little things can make a difference. A Bible that is reluctant to remain open or whose print is too small to read comfortably is clearly an impedance to concentration. We cannot sit still if our circumstances are uncomfortable. If we are alone we may find it useful to form the words as we read, even to the point of reading aloud—or at least reading quietly to ourselves. The sound of the words sometimes makes a greater impact on us than the mere visual form of the words on a page. Like poetry, a vocalized text has the power to move us at a deep level—far beneath and beyond the rational content of the text.

It is particularly important that we develop the skill of close reading, paying attention to every word, and allowing nothing to pass unnoticed. We will often discover that even after many years of reading a particular text we easily pass over some particular word or phrase that is important. In our formal education we may have been exposed to the imperative of reading quickly, and we may have acquired the habit of skimming through a text, grasping its major components but not paying much attention to everything. *Lectio* demands different skills. It requires the recognition that the text we are reading has been carefully crafted, sometimes—for example, in the case of the gospels—passing through several editorial stages before attaining its final form. We need to force ourselves to slow down, to pause, to reread. Perhaps we need to relearn the art of wondering. This is especially true when we are reading familiar texts. The danger is that we will simply re-engage with the text in terms of what we have already experienced, forgetting that each new day provides us with a vantage point from which new perspectives may appear.

Lectio divina is like painting a wall with a brush. We have to apply the paint evenly, going backwards and forwards and only slowly advancing beyond what is already done. We stop to listen for the echoes in our hearts—the mysterious conjunction of the words we are reading and the unspoken and unexpressed movements of our soul. *Lectio divina* is an important means of acquiring spiritual literacy, the ability to read what is happening in the depths of our being. This is what Saint Athanasius believed: "The Psalms are for those who recite them, as it were, a mirror in which the movements of the soul may be perceived."[9] So we read every verse or even every phrase several times before moving on. And the next day we read the same passage again, not only reviving the memory of what we have experienced previously, but seeking new insights into the sacred text.

9. *A Letter to Marcellinus*, §12, trans. Robert C. Gregg (New York: Paulist Press, 1980), 111.

It is leisureliness that is the hallmark of *lectio divina*. Although many people recommend using the liturgical readings of the day as the basis of *lectio*, this is not the monastic understanding of the practice. Nor is our time of *lectio* meant to provide an opportunity to prepare a homily. Useful though it is to meditate and pray around the liturgical readings, it compels one to keep moving forward as the readings change. There is the expectation that one will continue to move forward, even though there may be an interior summons to pause and extract the fullest meaning from a particular passage that reverberates strongly in the heart.

Lectio divina is a sapiential reading; the savor of the words is of its essence. There should be no pressure to cover a particular, predetermined amount of text, but the willingness to spend as much time as needed with even a short text. As Saint Benedict notes in RB 73.3, "What page or even what word of divine authority in the Old or New Testament is not a very direct guide for human life?" The spiritual meanings of the Bible are many and can provide us not only with challenging directives for our future conduct but also with solace when life is hard.[10] Pushing ahead to keep pace with the liturgical cycle may rob us of the possibility of drawing from the sacred text the deeper wisdom that will help guide us to a more abundant life.

Taking the biblical books seriously as literary compositions means that it is vital to read whole books rather than merely extracts or—even worse—individual verses taken out of context.[11]

10. "As a general rule, we can define the spiritual sense, as understood by Christian faith, as the meaning expressed by the biblical texts when read, under the influence of the Holy Spirit, in the context of the paschal mystery of Christ and of the new life which flows from it" (The Pontifical Biblical Commission, *The Interpretation of the Bible in the Church* II, B, 2 [Boston: St. Paul Books & Media, 1993], 85).

11. Sometimes Providence works through a kind of lucky dip when a random verse speaks powerfully to us—as in the case of the conversion of Antony, Augustine, and Alypius. Such providential interventions are not, strictly speaking, *lectio divina*.

Inspiration works its magic through human agencies. The books of the Bible are also the fruit of human industry. The authors examined sources both oral and written, they cooperated with others, and they carefully chose the form in which the message was to be communicated. We need to respect what they have done with so much deliberation. For example, we cannot divorce the paranetic chapters of exhortation in the Epistle to the Romans from its dogmatic considerations. Apocalyptic references in Saint Mark's thirteenth chapter need to be read in the context of the whole gospel and not interpreted in isolation. We can go further. To a certain extent, every part of the New Testament needs to be read in the light of the whole as it was received and perceived by those responsible for its creation. The sacred authors composed books: they intended the elements to sit side by side to complete and complement one another. That is why, as Saint Benedict recommends (RB 48.15), we read whole books through from beginning to end (*per ordinem ex integro legant*). We will find by experience that, if we take a gospel or an epistle or one of the prophetic books and spend six months or a year in its company, we are far more likely to penetrate its deeper levels of meaning than if we simply rush through it like an express train.

In speaking about the practice of *lectio divina* we need to be aware of cultural and generational differences. Many of the practical aspects that we associate with *lectio divina* developed within the ambience of the literary culture of Benedictine monasticism, characterized by the title of Jean Leclercq's book, *The Love of Learning and the Desire for God*. Those who have been educated in literary cultures have a familiarity and facility with reading, which has both advantages and disadvantages for *lectio*. It is easy for them to presume that it is the same kind of exercise as that which they have encountered in their years of education and in the exercise of their profession. In acquiring the art of sacred reading there may still be things for them to learn and, more probably, things to unlearn. On the other hand, for those who grow up in a predominantly oral culture, the experience of reading is often something of a strain. This will often make it a more conscious exercise for them, but they may quickly weary of it.

Some readers may feel drawn to engage in sacred reading in a language not their own, either because they belong to a community that uses a language different from their own, or because they choose to read in a language that is unfamiliar—whether it be a biblical language or some other. Reading in a foreign language slows down the process and requires more concentration, but, on the other hand, it is often less effective in generating responses at the level of emotion. As for the digital generation, they will find book-reading a very flat experience; they may well become bored with the unchanging sameness of every page and miss the stimulation of following hyperlinks to new horizons.

It is not prudent to assume that because someone knows how to read a book, they will necessarily understand what is involved in the practice of *lectio divina*. In the process of formation they need to be initiated into an integral understanding of *lectio*. This means reminding them that the Word of God is not only a source of comfort and a support for their prayer. Often it plays a prophetic role in pointing out areas that are in need of correction. God's word is a two-edged sword that penetrates the pious facade we hide behind and reaches into the depths of our conscience and beyond. Our *lectio divina* is not fulfilling its role if it does not occasionally call us to conversion—sometimes in major issues as well as in the details of daily interaction. This is especially important in multicultural communities and where there is no common etiquette for setting a person on the right track. External conformity may be achieved, but there is no corresponding upgrading of interior attitudes. If a correction causes undue shame, it will do more harm than good, and a less confrontational source of re-orientation will be needed. *Lectio divina* should be for us a primary agent in the integral formation of our conscience, and we should see it also as a necessary means of providing the same formation for those who happen to be in our care.

Why do we speak about *lectio divina* as an element in building a functional and fruitful community life? The short answer is that *lectio* not only provides each of us with a progressively concordant vision based on the gospels, but it also endows us with the energy we need to be able to handle the challenges of communal living creatively. We can look to *lectio* and *lectio*-related activities to provide us with the interior resources necessary to live as a community of persons whose lives are shaped by the Gospel. It is the prime energy source of spiritual living. Will-power and determination are insufficient. We need the grace of God. The grace of God will influence the choices we make only to the extent that we consent to being so directed. A wise abbot once remarked to me that during a season when extra work was needed and *lectio* time was reduced, community relations often became fraught. Just as we become listless if we skip meals, so we become spiritually limp if we allow ourselves to drift away from regular *lectio* and prayer.

Lectio has a significance beyond the devotional. Those of us who pursue the evangelical life, taking the Gospel as our guide (RB Prol. 21: *per ducatum evangelii*), are obliged to maintain a high level of vigilance to ensure that our way of life is concordant with the teaching of the New Testament. Unless the Gospel is really our rule of life, there is a suspicion that our whole religious life may come under the heading of self-willed religion, and not as a response to God's self-revealing. We may well have strong beliefs and values, but if they do not concord with those of the Gospel, they may well carry us away from the community. If we are to be of one heart and one mind we must have an agreed basis upon which our unity is built. Intimate familiarity with the gospels is particularly important for those to whom the governance of the community is entrusted so that they be "learned in the divine law" (RB 64.9); otherwise they will be shaping the community according to their own unevangelized preferences.

The fruit of *lectio divina* is an evangelized heart; if the hearts of all follow the Gospel as guide, then our communities will be both united and spiritually purposeful. To the extent that our minds and hearts are saturated with the New Testament, we will find there much that could serve as a charter for monastic communities. For example, passages like Ephesians 4:1–5:4 and Colossians

3:1-17 offer practical encouragement to our communities to follow the more excellent path of genuine charity, and you will hear echoes of these texts not only in the Rule of Saint Benedict, but also often in monastic sources.

A monastic culture that supports and encourages the lifelong practice of *lectio divina* will almost certainly build a good community—not a perfect community, but a community that so patiently tolerates inevitable weaknesses that it truly does become a family that has one heart and one mind.

4

What Ascends Must Converge

The title of this chapter is borrowed from Teilhard de Chardin, who used a similar expression in reference to the Omega Point. It also points to a significant reality in community life. As the spiritual quality of a group is intensified, so does the quality of the common life improve. It does not take much power of observation to conclude that the major fissures in community life are due to human weakness and to sin. As holiness increases, so weaknesses are reduced and rebellious impulses are restrained. Growth in patience makes us less reactive to the rampant idiocies around us. Authentic charity sows the seeds of empathy in us so that we are no longer threatened by differences. When holiness attains a critical mass in the community the common life poses fewer problems.

A prayerful community is usually able to surmount the normal challenges of living together in a restricted environment. Although growth in prayerfulness is a work of grace, those charged with the governance of the community can do much to encourage such an outcome. By competent formation in prayer both initially and in an ongoing context. By proactively encouraging a prayerful and reflective ambience in the monastery. By promoting a good level of spiritual literacy in the community so that conversations about the inner workings of prayer are facilitated. By good example giving witness to the primacy of prayer over other useful or delectable alternatives. Ultimately, however, the responsibility falls on each individual member of the community to ensure that their own commitment to prayer is real and practical. Prayerfulness in a group is built mostly from the bottom up, not from the top down; it is the result of sustained fidelity on the part of many members who, as it were, frequently inject prayer into the bloodstream of the community.

Because of the importance of individual practice to the wellbeing of the community, I believe that one of the tasks worth undertaking from time to time is to review our practice of personal prayer.[1] Of course, we spend quite a large amount of time every day in liturgical prayer, and I do not underestimate the importance of that. But there is a value to casting a critical eye on the time spent in personal prayer. I suggest that one reason for this is that our prayer gives us a good indication of how things are going in our life. As Saint John Climacus wrote, "Your prayer will soon show in what state you are. Theologians say that prayer is the monk's mirror."[2] If we don't like what we see, it is no good throwing away the mirror and buying a new one. If we don't like what we see we have to change.

The reason that, from time to time, we have to change the mood or format of our prayer is simply that prayer results from the interaction of our faith with the reality of the present situation. John Cassian concluded that "there are as many forms of prayer as there are states of soul":

> Prayer is fashioned anew from moment to moment according
> to the measure in which the mind is purified and according
> to the sort of situation in which it finds itself, whether this
> be the result of external contingencies or its own doing. It

1. There is a treatment of prayer parallel to what follows in Michael Casey, *Grace: On the Journey to God* (Brewster, MA: Paraclete Press, 2018), 85–123.

2. Saint John Climacus, *The Ladder of Divine Ascent* 28.34, trans. Muriel Heppell (London: Faber, 1959), 253.

is certain, moreover, that nobody is ever able to keep praying in the same way. Persons pray in one manner when they are cheerful and in another when they are weighed down by sadness or a sense of hopelessness. When they are flourishing spiritually their prayer is different from when they are oppressed by the extent of their struggles. They pray in one way when they are seeking pardon for their sins and in another when they are asking for some grace or virtue or for the elimination of a particular vice. Sometimes prayer is conditioned by compunction, occasioned by the thought of hell and the fear of judgment; at other times, it is aflame with hope and desire for the good things to come. Persons pray in one manner when they find themselves in dangerous straits and in another when they enjoy quiet and security. Prayer is sometimes illumined by the revelation of heavenly mysteries, but at other times one is forced to be content with the sterile practice of virtue and the experience of aridity.[3]

We might conclude from this text that one of the greatest obstacles to prayer is the attempt to repeat yesterday's prayer, instead of allowing prayer to create itself out of the elements of today's situation. This may well lead us to the conclusion that perhaps we need to ask whether our understanding of prayer is appropriate for the real situation in which we find ourselves today.

About fifty years ago, when I was younger and more intellectually athletic, I read very carefully the formidable phenomenological study of prayer by Canon Maurice Nédoncelle. The original French title was *Prière humaine, prière divine*, but it was published in English as *The Nature and Use of Prayer.*[4] At the very beginning of his study the author signals three inseparable elements to be found in all prayer:

---

3. Cassian, *Conferences* 9:8; SCh 54:48–49.
4. Translated by A. Manson (London: Burns & Oates, 1964).

a. All prayer is contemplative—that is, it presupposes a personal presence, even though, to some degree, it must always contend with the obstacle of distance.

b. All prayer is, at least implicitly, petitionary. We come before the overflowing bounty of God with empty hands. This requires of us the ability to speak our needs honestly and the recognition that our desires must give way before God's kindly providence.

c. All prayer demands dedication. The one who prays offers a gift, a pledge, an offering, a sacrifice. It costs us.

Perhaps we might ponder each of these aspects of prayer at greater length.

1. Prayer as Contemplative

When I emphasized the I-Thou character of *lectio divina,* it was to make the point that reading the Scriptures with the traditional monastic attitude becomes a means of opening ourselves to an encounter with God. Without such moments of personal union, reading the Bible is simply an intellectual exercise. It is important for us in speaking of contemplative prayer that we do not lose sight of its interpersonal character. It is more than a state of inward quiet or *nirvana*. This is merely a preliminary stage. Real prayer involves the experience of being brought into the presence of God, the intensity of which is determined by our spiritual capacity. This means that the experience becomes more profound, more moving, and more deeply personal as we make progress in holiness and in humanity.

Saint Augustine characterizes the movement of contemplation as being from the exterior to the interior and from being preoccupied with what is of this world to seeking the things that are above, where Christ is seated at the right hand of the Father. The soul "calls itself back from exterior things to those that are interior, and from those that are lower to those that are higher. And it says,

'Oh, praise the Lord, my soul.' "[5] There is a momentum in contemplation that subtly keeps drawing the soul to what is more spiritual. Saint Bernard often quotes the text of Saint Paul: "If we have known Christ according to the flesh, we know him thus no longer" (2 Cor 5:16). The important thing to remember is that though the contemplative journey may culminate in what is loftier than we can imagine, its beginnings are firmly within the sphere of common experience. Saint Bernard pointed out that the road to ecstasy begins with throwing off the tyranny of the self in everyday matters; in other words, contemplative ecstasy begins with standing aside from self-will in a grace-inspired gesture of detachment.[6]

Through baptism we have become sharers in the divine nature, members of God's household with the privilege of using the familiar address, Abba. It is as though thereafter we exist in a continual state of prayer, although this is pre-elective and below the threshold of consciousness. Prayer is possible because God is present to us. The problem is, as Saint Augustine frequently laments, that we are not often present to God. We allow our attention to be fixed elsewhere, often at the behest of subconscious desires. We seek for something that is already available. We do not have to ascend to the heavens or cross the seas to find God, as Deuteronomy 30:11-14 reminds us: God is already on our lips and in our hearts, calling out for a response.

Prayer is always a response. It is generated by a grace-driven spontaneity that cannot be manufactured unilaterally. We do not produce prayer. All we can do is to make room for it. We aim, as much as circumstances permit, to reduce alternative activities and preoccupations. The art of prayer is primarily the art of subtraction—addition may be initially helpful, but it becomes somewhat less important as time goes by, especially for those who are regular

---

5. Augustine, *On Psalm 145,* 5; CC 40:2108.

6. See Michael Casey, "In Pursuit of Ecstasy: Reflections on Bernard of Clairvaux's *De diligendo Deo," Monastic Studies* 16 (1985): 139–56.

in their practice of *lectio divina* and whose days are punctuated by the hours of the Work of God.

Prayer is not, therefore, primarily a technique: something that can be taught and learned. This is the lesson we learn from all the great masters of the spiritual life. We can develop organizational skills that enable us to include time for regular prayer in our daily schedule. We can close down the rampages of the "wild ghostly wits," as the author of *The Cloud of Unknowing* suggests. We can learn techniques of mental concentration and emotional quiet. These are, as it were, the setting of the kindling that can bring us to the point of prayer. Sometimes we have to work harder at this stage than at others. At this point we await the spark that will light the flame where, by the energy of the Holy Spirit, our faith makes the leap from the reality of our life into the heart of God.

Saint Bernard taught that the basic pre-condition for contemplation is that the person's will is aligned with God's: *conformatio voluntatis*.[7] Contemplation is the natural effect of a life lived in accordance with the Gospel, a life lived in love. Nor is this the work of a moment; semi-habitual moments of contemplation are reserved, for "one who not only lives for Christ, but has already done so for a long time."[8] Before the full flowering of the contemplative experience in heaven, Bernard envisages a long period of contemplative expectation, marked by sustained fervor and patience. This interval is not without its anticipatory moments, which may be compared to the smell that goes before the taste.[9] These moments of intensity (*intentio cordis* as in RB 52.4) are the epit-

7. See Michael Casey, *Athirst for God: Spiritual Desire in Bernard of Clairvaux's Sermons on the Song of Songs*, CS 77 (Kalamazoo, MI: Cistercian Publications, 1988), 289–96.

8. *Cui vivere Christus non tantum sit, sed et diu iam fuerit* (Bernard of Clairvaux, SC 57.1; SBOp 2:126).

9. "Simeon was a just man because he was waiting for the Christ and experienced him through a spiritual sense of smell, even though he had not done homage to him in the flesh. He was blessed in his waiting, and through the smell of waiting he arrived at the taste of contemplation" (SC 67.6; SBOp 2:192).

ome of selflessness.[10] The soul completely forgets itself. "The soul becomes so aware of the Word that it is no longer aware of itself."[11] Far from being a crowning achievement, contemplation is a total gift, reserved for those who are radically empty of self-will.

The notion that contemplation grows out of life is embedded in the word itself. At its heart is the Sanskrit root *temp*.[12] Apparently, its ancient meaning was a notch on a stick used for keeping count or measurement. Many words that begin with *temp-* retain some hint of measurement. *Temperature* measures heat, *tempo* measures musical time, *temperance* is the virtue that tempers or moderates our pleasures, *temperament* is a measure of our prevailing psychological attitude. A *template* is something that allows us to give a pre-decided form to what we are creating. Of particular interest is the word *temple*. Originally this referred to a measured area in the sky, and later came to signify a sacred precinct on earth that, in some way, mirrored the heavenly archetype. A prime example is Stonehenge, a prehistoric site of standing stones aligned with the position of the sun at significant times of the year. The purpose of a temple is to be, as it were, an outpost of heaven where believers may enter and find themselves in contact with ultimate reality. A temple is a celebration of con-formity, a zone on earth in which the laws of heaven are observed.

Contemplation is a state of being in accordance with God. It occurs in our life before it surfaces in our experience. Contemplation is what comes about when our interior division is overcome and we pass into a state in which our inner core is substantially

10. See Michael Casey, "*Intentio Cordis* (RB 52.4)," *Regulae Benedicti Studia* 6/7 (1977/1978): 105–21. Reprinted in Michael Casey, *An Unexciting Life: Reflections on Benedictine Spirituality* (Petersham, MA: St Bede's Publications, 2005), 335–58.

11. Bernard of Clairvaux, SC 85.13; SBOp 2:316.

12. I was alerted to this by David Steindl-Rast. See *Gratefulness, the Heart of Prayer: An Approach to Life in its Fullness* (New York: Paulist Press, 1984), 60–62.

undivided—what the ancient monks termed "purity of heart." In this emerging state of transparency God gradually appears. It is as though God is all the time outside the window of the soul. When the soul is purified, then, if we choose to look, we can catch sight of what had previously been unseeable. And sometimes God taps on the window. Contemplation is more something that happens than something that is done.

This is why Bernard often describes the state of contemplation as one of inaction. It is God's work, not ours:

> In his shadow I sit. To sit means to be quiet. It is a greater thing to rest in his shadow than simply to live in it, just as it is a greater thing to live in it merely than to exist in it.[13]

Bernard makes use of many terms already familiar from monastic vocabulary: *quies*,[14] *sedere*,[15] *securitas*,[16] *dormire*,[17] *vacare*,[18] and *otium*.[19] They are indicative of a state that is the opposite of activity. The author of *The Cloud of Unknowing* takes a similar approach in *The Epistle of Privy Counsel:*

> And well is this work likened to a sleep. For as in sleep the use of the bodily wits is ceased, that the body may take his full rest in feeding and strengthening of the bodily nature: right so in this ghostly sleep the wanton questions of the wild ghostly wits, imaginative reasons, be fast bound and utterly voided, so that the silly soul may softly sleep and rest in the lovely beholding of God as he is, in full feeding and strengthening of the ghostly nature.[20]

---

13. Bernard of Clairvaux, SC 48.8; SBOp 2:264.
14. Bernard of Clairvaux, SC 18.6; SBOp 1:107, etc.
15. Bernard of Clairvaux, SC 12.8; SBOp 1:65, etc.
16. Bernard of Clairvaux, SC 33.6; SBOp 1:238, etc.
17. Bernard of Clairvaux, SC 47.4; SBOp 2:64, etc.
18. Bernard of Clairvaux, SC 10.9; SBOp 1:53, etc.
19. Bernard of Clairvaux, Sent 3.121; SBOp 6b:229, etc.
20. *The Book of Privy Counsel* 152, chap. 6.

In another admonition, the author summarizes his understanding of the matter: "Keep on doing this nothing."[21]

Nothing on earth is loftier than contemplation, yet its beginnings are accessible to all believers—at least occasionally and for
a moment: *rara hora et parva mora.* All genuine prayer is contemplative, because it presupposes contact with God. It may not
reach the depths of intensity that the mystics experienced, but
there is a real and life-giving encounter that becomes a means of
ongoing transformation as the person becomes more and more
conformed to Christ, and more effective in drawing others to follow the same course.

2. Prayer as Petitionary

Truth is the basis of prayer. When I come into the presence of
the Holy One I am immediately confronted by my own unworthiness. Or, perhaps, it is the other way around. When I consider my
extreme neediness I am driven to seek a solution beyond myself.
Since I am the source of that which causes my shame, I cannot
be its solution. I have to seek elsewhere. This is the conclusion at
which Saint Augustine arrived: "Because I am human, therefore
I am weak. Because I am weak, therefore I pray."[22] Self-knowledge
leads to a heightened sense of dependence on the grace of God.
When I have become aware of how lacking I am in personal integrity, my faith generates a heartfelt cry: "O God, come to my
assistance. O Lord, make haste to help me." My whole life is in
need of forgiveness, cleansing, healing, re-alignment, liberation,
and it is these great gifts for which I ask, even when I seem to be
seeking something more mundane and trivial.

As was indicated in the text from John Cassian quoted above,
there is a prayer for every season of our life. Saint Bernard notes

---

21. "Bot trauayle besily in that nouwt" (*The Cloud of Unknowing*, 122, chap.
68).

22. Saint Augustine, *On Psalm 29.2*, 1; CC 38:174.

that there is a tidal change in the predominant emphasis as we make progress in the spiritual life:

> There are four degrees of prayer along with their respective feelings. The first is when a human being enters the way of God and, like Job, prays against evil habit, and desires to be delivered from the trap of the customary depravity in which his foot is caught. Secondly, once liberated from bad habit, he dares to ask pardon for his sins. Thirdly, after pardon, he prays that the virtues be given him and he also prays on behalf of others. Fourthly, he thus becomes so familiar with God that, whenever he prays, he tends more to give thanks than to make petitions.[23]

As this text seems to indicate, prayer expands. Although prayer seems to have intensely personal beginnings, it is not for long locked within solipsistic concerns. Informed by the dual command of love that dictates the combination of vertical and horizontal dimensions, even as prayer reaches out to God, it also gradually expands its embrace to include other people and, eventually, the whole of creation.

The first letter of Pope Clement I (the *Prima Clementis*) already proclaims the universal extension of all genuine prayer:

> We ask you, Master, to become our helper and defender. Save those of us who are in trouble, have mercy on the lowly, raise up the fallen, manifest yourself to the needy, heal the sick, correct those of your people who are in error, satisfy the hungry, ransom those of us who are captives, lift up the weak, console those who are pusillanimous. May all nations come to know you, that you alone are God and Jesus Christ is your Child and we are your people, the sheep of your pasturing.[24]

---

23. Bernard of Clairvaux, Sent 3.101; SBOp 6b:168.

24. Clement I, *Prima Clementis* 59.4, trans. Bart D. Ehrman, in *The Apostolic Fathers,* vol. 1 (Cambridge, MA: Harvard University Press, 2003), 142.

In a sense, all prayer is directed to the coming of God's ultimate kingdom. My deeply felt appeal for help becomes the voice of all humanity. In an instruction to an anchoress, sometimes thought to have been his sister, Aelred of Rievaulx encourages her to reach out to embrace the entire world with the arms of her prayer:

> In a single act of love hold the whole world in your heart. There consider all the good people together and rejoice. There look upon the evil and lament. Gaze upon those in trouble and oppressed and share their suffering. Within your soul encounter the wretchedness of the poor, the wailing of orphans, the desolation of widows, the grief of those who mourn, the troubles of travelers, the dangers of those at sea, the offerings of virgins, the temptations of monks, the cares of prelates, the labor of soldiers. Open to all the breast of your love. Let your tears flow for them. Pour out your prayers for them.[25]

Saint Bernard, likewise, notes that there is a certain large-heartedness (*amplo affectu*) in true prayer, so that even in the act of praying for oneself, others are also included.[26]

I cannot truthfully come before God without, by that very fact, recognizing my dependence on God. In an intense I-Thou relationship there is no scope for dissimulation. To hide my negativities from God is to hide myself behind the bluster of many words (*multiloquium*) such as Jesus condemned. Just as we know that, in ordinary human interchange, language can be used not only to communicate but also to interpose a barrier to communication, so saying prayers cannot be a substitute for entering into a relationship with God. Such words are meant to maintain control, to keep God at a distance. That is probably why Martin Luther recommended "Few words but many meanings," and ancient monasticism arrived at the formula that prayer should be brief but frequent. A single glance is all God needs to assess and accept the reality

25. Aelred of Rievaulx, *De institutione inclusarum* 28; CCCM 1:661–62.
26. Bernard of Clairvaux, Div 107.1; SBOp 6a:379.

of our situation; for us the process takes much longer. To appear shamelessly naked before God demands a great deal of confidence in God's pre-emptive and unconditional welcome.

Because Jesus has revealed to us that God is our Father, we may well conclude that our personal prayer should be both intimate and uninhibited. The Psalmist reminds us that God knows the dust of which we are made and does not expect superhuman efforts of us either in our life or in our prayer. God does not limit relationships to high achievers. When we come before God, we become conscious of the liabilities that we carry, and these may well provide us with the starting point for our prayer: "Lord, I am distracted by a thousand frivolities." "Forgive me, Lord, for I have sinned." "Lord, I have a headache and I think I am developing a cold." "Lord, I am bitter and very angry." The great gift is to be able freely to bring these burdens into awareness and to allow the healing flood of divine acceptance to wash over us.

3. Prayer as Dedication

Despite the limpid simplicity of Saint Benedict's admonition—"Let him simply enter and pray" (*simpliciter intret et oret*: RB 52.4)—most of us experience prayer as being a little more complicated than that. Perseverance in daily prayer is not easy. If prayer were not a challenge, it would not be necessary for us to spend time reflecting on it. A prayerful life demands much dedication and even a certain degree of doggedness if we are to persevere in its practice. If people did not find prayer demanding, why was Eugene Boylan's 1943 book, *Difficulties in Mental Prayer,* a bestseller?[27]

What difficulties are we likely to encounter in our own efforts to live a more prayerful life? I am taking it for granted that we

---

27. Eugene Boylan, *Difficulties in Mental Prayer* (Dublin: Gill and Macmillan, 1943; new ed. Ave Maria Press, 2010).

lead an ordinary life and that we participate in the liturgy and are moderately faithful to the various observances that are meant to provide some support for a life of prayer.

a. There are no measurable outcomes in prayer. The rules of cause and effect do not seem to apply. We can never know in advance what is going to happen, and our sessions of prayer rarely pass as we had planned. Since the reward of tangible results does not attach to our efforts, we are less motivated to continue.

b. There seems never to be enough time in the day to include prayer. As *The Cloud of Unknowing* states as long back as the fourteenth century, "Nothing is more precious than tyme."[28] Work expands to fill most of the time available, and relaxation devours the rest. The time for prayer is often abrogated or curtailed. Notwithstanding the ancient monks' stated (though rarely—if ever—realized) ideal of continuous prayer, the most feasible solution is often to make a rule for ourselves—a rule within the common rule—so that there is some chance of avoiding the virtual disappearance of prayer from our life. We would do well to follow the recommendation of Abbot John Chapman of Downside:

> The only way to pray is to pray; and the way to pray well is to pray much. If one has no time for this, then one must, at least, pray regularly. But the less one prays, the worse it goes.[29]

c. Prayer brings with it the challenge of self-knowledge and demands of us the progressive abandonment of many cherished illusions. We are sometimes made painfully aware of the shallowness of our piety and the precariousness of our virtue. The advantage

---

28. "& perforce take good keep into tyme, how that thou dispendist it. For nothing is more precious than tyme" (*The Cloud of Unknowing*, 20, chap. 4).

29. Dom Roger Hudleston, ed., *The Spiritual Letters of Dom John Chapman* (London: Sheed & Ward, 1935), 53.

of this is that it slowly leads us to appreciate that prayer is not doing God a favor but is entirely for our benefit, leading us into a fuller truth and a sincerer humility.

d. Sad to say, although others may consider us to be experts in prayer and to be very well educated in spiritual matters, we do not always have a theory of prayer that speaks to our own evolving experience. It sometimes helps to read something about prayer in order to update our theory so that it speaks to our current situation.

e. Sometimes we can be tyrannized by practices, methods, or techniques that seemed to work in the past. We persevere doggedly in using them even though they seem to be of little help. Probably we need the boldness to experiment with different ways of engaging with prayer, until we find means of easing the blankness that we are currently experiencing.

f. If we follow the schema promulgated by Saint John of the Cross, we can expect to pass through two "nights" as we make our way up the mountain. These pose a special problem for many who are resistant to the idea that their prayer is changing and try to keep it the same. For most people the best thing they can do is to let it happen, without trying to seize control. In the absence of contrary indications, the wisest course is to do nothing.

g. John Cassian makes the point that our prayer is conditioned by what has been passing through our minds outside the time of prayer. Some effort at eliminating contrary imaginations during the day will probably impact positively on what happens during the time of prayer. Sometimes it helps to glide gradually into prayer, creating a buffer zone in which potential distractions are eased out of our minds.

h. Prayer is also bedeviled by serious moral inconsistencies in our behavior. Richard Sipe, a psychologist who has treated many priests experiencing substantial difficulties with celibacy, has found that the absence of an honest prayer life is either the cause or the effect of their moral collapse:

In studying religious celibacy for thirty-five years I have never found one exception to this fundamental rule: Prayer is necessary to maintain the celibate process. A neglectful prayer life ensures the failure of celibate integration. No matter at what point in or out of the celibate process you find yourself, if you really want to be celibate, you can begin today by praying.[30]

This is one instance that demonstrates the truth of the saying, "If your prayer stinks, it is because your life stinks."

The fact that our prayer is unsatisfactory or unsatisfying is no reason to discontinue the practice. But perseverance in what seems to be a fruitless exercise demands a good measure of patience and a strong faith in the power of even the most seemingly hopeless prayer. Here we may be encouraged by words put into the mouth of Christ by Julian of Norwich:

> Pray with your whole being even though you think that it has no savor for you. For such prayer is very profitable even though you feel nothing. Pray with your whole being, though you feel nothing, though you see nothing, even though it seems impossible to you. It is in dryness and in barrenness, in sickness and in feebleness that your prayer is most pleasing to me, even though you think that it has little savor for you.[31]

Anything that we can do—no matter how small—to give more scope to prayer in our lives is worthwhile and, supposing we persevere in it, will certainly yield dividends in due season.

---

30. A. W. Richard Sipe, *Celibacy: A Way of Loving, Living, and Serving* (Alexandria, Australia: E. J. Dwyer, 1996), 54.

31. Translated from *Revelations* 14.41 (Edmund Colledge and James Walsh, ed., *A Book of Showings to the Anchoress Julian of Norwich* [Toronto: Pontifical Institute of Mediaeval Studies, 1978], 464–65).

The trajectory traced out in Saint Benedict's seventh chapter is clear. The initial priority in the spiritual journey is to abandon the state of irresponsibility and to begin to pay more attention to the quality of one's life. To offset the dire effects of mindlessness we need to become mindful of "all that God has commanded," fleeing from all forgetfulness (RB 7.11-12), because forgetfulness is the death of the soul. A lifetime of care and concern about turning aside from evil and doing good leads to a state in which good habits govern one's existence and the drama of struggling against contrary inclinations is diminished. The monk is beginning to pass beyond a busy mindfulness to a state beyond mindfulness in which, without adverting to obligations and responsibilities, he is simply aware of living under the merciful gaze of God. Wherever he is, and in whatever occupation he is engaged, he discovers that the state of continual prayer of which the ancients spoke is beginning to find a home in his heart. It is this overwhelming presence of God that brings about the most complete state of self-knowledge and, therefore, of humility. Of this important topic we will have more to say later.

5

Responsiveness to Persons

If there is any lesson to be learned from our exposure to the New Testament it is the importance and dignity of every person and the consequent obligation of Christian communities and institutions to be not only accepting of persons in all their uniqueness, but sincerely cherishing each as a particular manifestation of the glory of God. And if the glory of God is to be found in the fully alive human being, as Saint Irenaeus taught, then we are all obliged to make every effort to ensure that the members of our community reach the highest possible attainment of their potential.

"The human person was not made for the Sabbath, but the Sabbath was made for the human person." This principle holds for all religious institutions, even the noblest. The value of such institutions is to be measured by the ultimate benefit they communicate to those involved in them. Human persons are not pieces on a chessboard, to be moved around at the behest of another for some ulterior purpose. They are imbued by nature with a certain *dignitas*—of themselves they are inherently worthwhile. In the words used by the former President of Ireland, Mary Robinson, as the title for her memoirs, *Everybody Matters*.[1]

---

1. London: Hodder & Stoughton, 2012.

"Charity begins at home"—but it is only the beginning. If the monastery is to be considered a school of love, *schola dilectionis*, it is not only because the monks and nuns really love one another. The hospitality they extend to other members of the community necessarily reaches out beyond the cloister to guests, to those for whom we have pastoral responsibility, to strangers, and to all with whom we come into contact. Wholehearted followers of the monastic way ought to be the most respectful people, with no frontiers imposed on those to whom this respect is given.

Since the European Enlightenment of the seventeenth and eighteenth centuries, the theme of human dignity and of universal human rights is sometimes thought to be a modern idea, perhaps with its roots in the ancient civilizations of Greece and Rome. Larry Siedentop has submitted this proposition to a painstaking examination. He rejects the notion that the idea of the natural equality of all persons can be traced to the classical world and concludes that it derives from the New Testament, from the teaching of Jesus as elaborated by Saint Paul:[2]

> Paul's conception of the Christ overturns the assumption on which ancient thinking had hitherto rested, the assumption of natural inequality. Instead, Paul wagers on human equal-

---

2. Professor John Gray, himself an atheist, states a similar proposition at the beginning of his book *Seven Types of Atheism* (London: Allen Lane, 2018), 1: "Modern liberalism is a late flower of Jewish and Christian religion." And, "By remaking religion as a form of belief—a matter of conscience, not just ritual observance—Christianity created a demand for freedom that did not exist in the ancient world. Valuing inward worship more than public practice, the early Christians set in motion a movement that would culminate in the creation of a secular realm" (18). In a concordant conclusion, Tom Holland writes, "To live in a Western country is to live in a society still utterly saturated by Christian concepts and assumptions. . . . Even to write about it in a Western language is to use words shot through with Christian connotations. . . . The West, increasingly empty though the pews may be, remains firmly moored to its Christian past" (*Dominion: The Making of the Western Mind* [London: Little Brown, 2019], xxv).

ity. It is a wager that turns on transparency, that we can and should see ourselves in others, and others in ourselves.[3]

This insight into human equality led to the Christian church's becoming inclusive in its outreach—it was not limited to a particular class of people, but baptism was open to all, and persons from different backgrounds were invited to share eucharistic fellowship. This egalitarian tendency did not, however, lead to tyrannical uniformity. On the contrary, the harmony realized by inclusion made a certain pluralism inevitable and, thereby, an emphasis on inwardness more feasible.[4] Conversely, the more persons went beyond the superficial, the more possible it became to accept differences in others and to live in peace. This connection between depth of interior life and depth of community is worth noting. We all need to arrive at a dynamic balance between extraversion and introversion. We need to arrive at the point of recognition that it is impossible to achieve substantial long-term harmony in community without a deep interior life. Social dynamics that attempt to "build community" without paying attention to the quality of the inner life of each will inevitably fall short of the ideal.[5]

3. Larry Siedentop, *Inventing the Individual: The Origins of Western Liberalism* (London: Penguin Books, 2015), 60.

4. "The basilicas built in Rome by the Emperor Constantine, after his conversion in 312, gave architectural expression to the difference of focus between paganism and the new moral beliefs. In place of the ancient temple, with its splendid columns and decorations on the exterior, the Christian basilica was simple, unadorned brick on the outside, with columns and decorations reserved for the interior. The change was symptomatic. Where paganism had concerned itself primarily with external conformity of behaviour, Christianity concerned itself especially with inner conviction" (Siedentop, *Inventing*, 89).

5. Just as attempting to grow in the love of God without simultaneously growing in the love and service of the neighbor is futile. This is why Basil (*Long Rules* §7; trans. Anna Silvas, *The Asketikon of St Basil the Great* [Oxford: Oxford University Press, 2005], 180–86) and Pachomius (*Bohairic Life* §105; trans. Armand Veilleux, *Pachomian Koinonia: Volume One*, CS 45 [Kalamazoo, MI: Cistercian Publications, 1980], 149) thought cenobites superior to hermits.

The monastic movements of the early centuries embodied both the recognition of the dignity of each person and the value of Christian community. They were open to those excluded from participation in civic life—notably women, the lower classes, and slaves. Then, "as hermits or anchorites became cenobites—that is, as asceticism became communal—Christian beliefs began to generate a new conception of 'community,' an utterly new form of social organization."[6] The role of individual conscience, operating within the bounds of a universal moral law, became paramount. Cenobites associated voluntarily—a group formed on the basis of individual choice. From this it follows that "the form of a community consistent with equality of souls was essentially a community of shared values."[7] In this conception rules were essentially freely accepted and internalized, and the superior, who was chosen by the community and not imposed,[8] governed not according to his own preferences but in accordance with the common body of beliefs and values:

> Benedict's Rule reinforced the democratizing of the idea of authority, insisting that monastic leaders temper their government with a "listening" culture and respect the different needs of individual monks. The object was "to work towards the fellow citizenship of the heavenly kingdom." To promote such moral equality, Benedict sought to eliminate social distinctions within the monastery.[9]

6. Siedentop, *Inventing,* 93. See also 95: "Separating themselves physically as well as morally from the ancient family and the polis, monks offered the picture of a world founded on different principles."

7. Siedentop, *Inventing,* 96.

8. It has to be noted that Benedict is open to the possibility that an abbot could be elected by a *pars sanior* of the community instead of by the unanimous choice of the whole community (RB 64.1). Today a majority vote of the community is usual, and, as a result, in top-heavy communities, a candidate is sometimes swept to power by the infirmary vote, perhaps to the chagrin of the more active members of the community.

9. Siedentop, *Inventing,* 97.

The principle that determines relationships within the community is honor. "The basis for peace in the Rule of Benedict is not merely a desire, nor frictionless, successful, and effective functioning, but rather the honor and dignity for each person which the Rule enjoins."[10] It is easy to pass the word *honor* without giving it much attention. It is, however, a significant component of fruitful community interaction.[11] Honor stands as the culmination of a threefold positive response to others. As a foundation, we must treat others with civility and **politeness**, seasoned with an appropriate measure of deference. Then we must give them **respect**, recognizing their particular gifts and talents, their years of commitment, and their ongoing contribution to the community. Ultimately we **honor** them, appreciating their inherent dignity as human beings created in the image and likeness of God. We affirm them not only for the good that they **do**, but also for the good that they **are**. This obligation applies to all the members of a community, but is particularly important in the exercise of the ministry of authority:

> Benedict considered authority only justifiable and good when official power was . . . combined with respect for individuality, different abilities, and particular personal needs. . . . He understands authority as an instance that helps, supports, encourages, and exhorts, and is constantly mindful of the progress and welfare of those who are subject

---

10. Translated from Michaela Puzicha, "Benedikt von Nursia: Botschaft und Aktualiktät im 21. Jahrhundert—Vier Aspekte," in Jürgen Henkel and Nikolaus Wyrwoll, ed., *Askese versus Konsumgesellschaft: Aktualität und Spiritualität von Mönchtum und Ordensleben im 21. Jahrhundert* (Bonn: Schiller Verlag, 2013), 107.

11. See Michael Casey, "The Role of Honouring Others in Benedictine Leadership," *Benedictines* 73, no. 1 (2020): 22–28; "Benedictine Education: Two Words," *Tjurunga* 93 (2020): 15–31. There is a useful excursus on how honor was understood in ancient Mediterranean societies in John Dominic Crossan, *The Historical Jesus: The Life of a Mediterranean Jewish Peasant* (North Blackburn, Australia: Collins Dove, 1991), 9–15.

to it. The purpose of real authority is therefore always to help people to become more independent and discover what lies within their capabilities: in other words, help them to become free.[12]

In contrast to situations marked by a depersonalizing zeal for efficiency, through technology and bureaucracy—and the consequent possibilities for exploitation and abuse—monasteries in the Benedictine tradition are called to be safe places where human beings can live and grow. Islands of humanity. This means that social goals are subordinated to the growth of persons and their communion with others, and it involves especially the practical enabling and empowering of persons, facilitating growth, and providing opportunities for self-actualization. This growth operates at several levels but is oriented toward spiritual flowering, openness to the spiritual world, union with God, contemplation.

Benedict notes that an abbot who governs souls with genuine respect for their dignity has been given a difficult task (RB 2.31). This does not make it less necessary. The implications of such an approach are made explicit in Gregory the Great's *Pastoral Rule*, a text highly recommended by Pope John Paul I to bishops who visited him during his brief tenure of office. In a series of thirty-four chapters in the third part of this work, Saint Gregory offers guidance for differential pastoral practice. Somewhat repetitively he speaks of how to admonish the poor and the rich, the joyful and the sad, the wise and the dull, the married and the celibate, and many others. One size does not fit all.[13] The point he makes over and over again is that virtue usually occupies the middle ground between contrary vices—those at both ends of the spectrum are to be encouraged to move toward the center, even though the direction of movement of one is the exact opposite of the other.

12. Notker Wolf and Enrica Rosanna, *The Art of Leadership* (Collegeville, MN: Liturgical Press, 2013), 5.

13. See *St. Gregory the Great: Pastoral Care,* trans. Henry Davis, ACW 11 (Westminster: The Newman Press, 1950).

The same delicacy is to be hoped for in the mutual relations among the members of the community. Their attitudes to one another need to be grounded on the expectation that others are legitimately and appropriately different, and that these inherent differences are worthy of honor. It is only when persons are confident that they are accepted, appreciated, and loved for what they are that it becomes possible slowly to create a community that is both effective and affective. On the other hand, a community riven by favoritism, factions, and feuds will inevitably fall apart.

A community needs to nurture a sense of belonging together that is much, much stronger than fellow travelers on a bus or airplane experience. Community is more than occupying the same space or living in the same building, or moving in the same direction. It involves some level of bonding so that persons feel at home in the community, comfortable, relaxed, creative, original. For this to happen, it is necessary to build a good level of mutual trust based on a confidence that others are looking out for one's welfare. Mutuality consists in living in the context of others; it is the opposite of self-will. It is the acceptance of the priority of the common will.[14] Growth in mutuality can be seen in progressive movement from selfishness to greater sensitivity, from conflict to harmony or, at least, to resolution of differences, from stalemate to effective dialogue and purposeful community action, from obstinacy to openness to persuasion and adaptability, from aggression to patience, and from withdrawal to participation. The ultimate outcome is that dysphoria is replaced by euphoria; people feel better about living in this particular community—notwithstanding its many failings.

A community in which mutuality flourishes is not a community of clones. There are very few monastic communities that are deprived of the benefit of eccentric characters.[15] This is because there

14. See Michael Casey, "Merton's Teaching on the 'Common Will' and What the Journals tell Us," *The Merton Annual* 12 (1999): 62–84.

15. See the remark made by Guillaume Jedrzejczak, former abbot of Mont-de-Cats: "Sometimes it is thought that monasteries are places of uniformity,

is respect for differences—differences in personality, culture, talent, education, official status, and, above all, differences in spirituality. And a willingness to be amused rather than irritated. Sister Helen Lombard spoke about "a community of unequals"— persons are equal in dignity and acceptance, but different. Each is unique:

> I believe that "the good zeal that monks ought to have" (RB 72) is to be exercised always in a community of unequals, a community of the weak and the strong, of some with one gift and others another, of those who need more and those who need less, of the advanced and less advanced in the monastic way of life. All are radically one in Christ (2.20), all are brothers to one another within the community. Yet the community is complex, messy, diverse. Each member has a specific place within it. Relationships are not perfectly symmetrical. There is nothing smoothly egalitarian about it at all. It is in such a community of unequals that the brothers are called to practise obedience with the warmest love (72.3).[16]

This means that there is scope for each to exercise an active and generative care for the well-being of the community:

> Every member of the community, by virtue of his age and seniority, plays a part in the educative role which in tradi- tional coenobitism was reserved to the abbot and to the office-holders. The chapter "On Good Zeal" attributes even more generously to the life of charitable fraternal relation- ships, the purifying and sanctifying effects which the Master

---

whereas in reality they are probably the places on the planet where you can find the highest number of eccentrics per square meter." Quoted in Dysmas de Las- sus, *Risques et dérives de la vie religieuse* (Paris: Cerf, 2020), 120.

16. Helen Lombard, SGS, "Mutual Obedience: An Aborted Effort?—Chapter 71," *Tjurunga* 53 (1997): 74.

saw as the result of asceticism lived under the abbot's direction.[17]

When Benjamin Chaminade, a business consultant, sought to find what quality enabled enterprises to retain their most valued employees, he discovered that the key to retention was what he termed *fidélisation*. A mutual loyalty is established when the talents of all are recognized, appreciated, utilized, and encouraged to develop:

> *Fidélisation* is the voluntary action by which a business establishes an environment that maintains the attachment of the employee over a long period. This enduring and constant attachment that binds the employee to the business is based on shared values. Putting in place a policy of *fidélisation* consists in placing persons and their expectations at the heart of the business concerns so that the professional satisfaction of the employee is assured and a relationship of mutual confidence is established.[18]

The lesson for monastic communities is that we have to be active in earning, securing, and growing the trust not only of those who enter but of all the members of a community.[19] This is done especially through good communication, sustained listening, proactive involvement, and fair dealing. And a certain open-hearted and gratuitous friendliness. In particular, building trust means dealing honestly and creatively with any grievances that arise, and preventing the emergence of any chronic sense of alienation that might push individuals or groups toward the margins of the community.

17. Adalbert de Vogüé, *Community and Abbot in the Rule of Saint Benedict*, CS 5/2 (Kalamazoo, MI: Cistercian Publications, 1988), 430–31.

18. Benjamin Chaminade, "Fidélisation versus retention," 8 June 2003, translated from www.focusrh.com/article.php3?id_article=107.

19. See Michael Casey, "Building Trust," in *The Art of Winning Souls: Pastoral Care of Novices* (Collegeville, MN: Liturgical Press, 2012), 110–34.

It may well be that some members of the community contribute more to the realization of the community's overt goals and objectives, but all members of a community have the right to be valued equally—even if they seem to be non-contributory, such as the infirm, the aged, and the very new. The large stones in a building are the most obvious, but it is the mortar that holds them together. Without mortar the stones would tumble to the ground. A community can gratefully accommodate a few shining stars, but it urgently needs a mass of more humdrum people to ensure that the stars do not collide and cause the whole system to explode.

If good people are not happy then it is incumbent on all, but especially on those with pastoral responsibility, to uncover the reasons for this. This means being prepared to listen, and to keep listening when what is heard is unwelcome. Obviously this is more than "sponge-listening"—stoically enduring what may be perceived as a self-justifying monologue. It means really listening not only to the words that are uttered but also attending to the feelings from which they spring and the undoubtedly complicated history in which they are embedded.[20] It means imposing a moratorium on all defensiveness and judgment, and leaving oneself open and vulnerable. Persons who entrust their self-humiliating stories to another usually experience some measure of relief and consolation when their revelations are met with calmness and acceptance. When the result is irritated reluctance to hear more, the sense of alienation is heightened. Communities in which the ministry of listening is flourishing are generally happy communities. It is worth noting that such a service of listening is not limited to those who hold an office in the community—it is a gift that any can bestow.

It has been argued that the prime indicator of moral progress is inclusivity.[21] As a genuine moral sense develops it extends the focus of its gaze: from self to family to clan to tribe to nation to

20. See Michael Casey, "Integral Listening," in *Benedictines* 71, no. 2 (2018): 6–11.

21. See Allen Buchanan and Russell Powell, *The Evolution of Moral Progress: A Biocultural Theory* (New York: Oxford University Press, 2018).

all humanity to all living beings to the whole cosmos. From a very young age and without much prompting, empathy and altruism make an appearance with regard to others in one's own in-group. Growing up, outsiders are often considered threatening. Inclusivist moral responses, reaching out beyond these natural and cultural frontiers, depend partly on the cultural ambience and partly on deliberate choices. Offering hospitality to those who are different can become a way of life, but it is never automatic.

In communities made up of persons of different generations and different cultures, misunderstandings can often multiply, especially when there is no forum in which grievances can be aired creatively. It is not sufficient for the different cultures to co-exist without overt conflict; it is important that they interact so that multiculturality slowly becomes interculturality, with due honor paid to all its constitutive cultural forms. The difficulties involved in becoming truly intercultural are considerable, but so are the rewards.[22] This positive outcome will not happen if the culture of the community remains static and stagnant and the leadership lacks empathy or verve.

A similar expanded sensitivity is demanded in our dealings with the elderly, afflicted as they often are with bodily decrepitude or mental degradation.[23] Saint Benedict expects that the seniors will

22. See Anthony Gittins, *Living Mission Interculturally: Faith, Culture, and the Renewal of Praxis* (Collegeville, MN: Liturgical Press, 2015); Gerald A. Arbuckle, *Culture, Inculturation, and Theologians: A Postmodern Critique* (Collegeville, MN: Liturgical Press, 2010).

23. In a riff on Eccl 12:3-6, which he interprets as metaphor, Rabbi Rami Shapiro paints the following picture of old age. "Your eyes grow dim with cataracts. . . . [There are problems with] Your teeth. Your eyes. You cannot move your bowels. Your digestion is poor. You cannot sleep through the night for all the noise, yet you cannot hear people speaking to you during the day. Your balance is wobbly, and you fear stumbling over any uneven surface. Your nerves are so sensitive that almost anything causes irritation. Your spinal column loses all flexibility, and your back is in spasm. You fall and crack your skull. You suffer from vomiting and acid reflux. You become incontinent" (*Ecclesiastes: Annotated & Explained* [Nashville: Skylight Paths, 2016], 104–6).

be venerated (RB 4.70) and honored (RB 63.1), and he makes
provision for their special needs (RB 37). It needs to be said, however, that the elderly are not simply beneficiaries of the community's
good will. They have something to contribute. Good advice (RB
3.21) and spiritual support (RB 27.2-3) certainly. They also help to
maintain an even keel in the community when issues have the potential to rock the boat dangerously and cause disaster. The ability
to perceive recurrent patterns without the labor of detailed analysis
means that even without a pristine brain, many elderly persons are
able to sum up a situation and discern a solution with a minimum
of fuss: "Though the brain may age and change, each phase of this
progression presents new and different pleasures and advantages,
as well as losses and trade-offs, in a natural progression, like the
seasons."[24] "Genius (and talent) are usually associated with youth.
Wisdom and competence are the fruits of maturity. . . . Wisdom
and competence are the rewards of aging."[25] By the same token, the
seniors need to respect and make use of the specific talents of the
young, not only their ingenuity, persistence, and energy, but also
the likelihood that they are more competent in getting results from
ever-changing technology.

We should be in no doubt about the magnitude of the challenge
that the acceptance of difference involves, irrespective of whether it
involves fusion between cultures or generations. Embedded customs
resist change. The Vatican document *New Wine in New Wineskins*
states clearly that, in large measure, we have not successfully made
the transition into a new paradigm of consecrated life but, instead,
are clinging fearfully to the ragged remnants of former observances.
Continuing stubbornly to do the things that used to work is a totally
inadequate and uncreative response to necessary change:

> We must not be afraid to honestly acknowledge how, despite
> a series of changes, the old traditional framework struggles

---

24. Elkhonon Goldberg, *The Wisdom Paradox: How Your Mind Can Grow
Stronger as Your Brain Grows Older* (New York: Gotham Books, 2005), 10.
25. Goldberg, *The Wisdom Paradox*, 80.

to give way to new models in a decisive manner. Perhaps the entire constellation of languages and models, values and duties, spirituality and ecclesial identity that we are used to has not yet left room for the testing and stabilizing of the new paradigm born of inspiration and post-conciliar practice. . . . We must also indicate and interpret that tenacious resistance that had been hidden for a long time, but has now reappeared explicitly in many contexts even as a possible response to an ill-concealed sense of frustration. . . . As we are used to the taste of *old* wine and reassured by proven modalities, we are not really open to any change unless it is substantially irrelevant.[26]

Sometimes it seems that the smaller the issue the greater the emotional turmoil it engenders. The most obvious example of cultural variation, which has to be faced several times each day, concerns meals. What food is to be provided for community meals? And how is it to be served? Is it to be eaten with chopsticks, with fork and spoon, with knife and fork, with fingers? Hardly world-changing matters, but unless they are sensitively navigated, they have the possibility of leading to disproportionate reactions. Another example. The use of social media will be a point of contention between generations; the newly entered young will be puzzled by the reserve and resistance of some of their elders and, perhaps, incensed by any restrictions placed on their use of digital media. This also is a cultural gap that must be bridged sensibly and sensitively.

To give due honor to the different cultures of members of the community, an effort must be made to build a specific common culture that draws from all its constitutive elements but is identical to none. An all-embracing and inclusive sub-culture that honors all the elements that constitute the whole. A monastic subculture is created when monks and nuns strive to craft common forms for their life together. The end product combines different cultural

26. *New Wine*, §9.

strands, but in a healthy situation the drift will always be toward the local over the exotic. To produce such a fusion involves work in seven different areas.

History: An effort needs to be made to create an inclusive institutional memory. This will include not only the remote origins of the monastic community, but also the vicissitudes that have marked subsequent centuries, and the particularities of the local community. A consciousness of local and recent history is also important, as well as an acknowledgement of the stories that each member of the community brings to the common fund of shared identity.

Significant Persons: Within this history there are not only events but significant persons who have played a role in making the community what it is today. This will include the celebration of the feasts of the saints, but also an awareness of other persons who have contributed to the founding and growth of the community. This includes deceased members of the community, appropriately remembered by means of a necrology, and visits to the cemetery. I was impressed once when I visited a community that had photographs of its deceased members on the wall—as though affirming that they remained part of the community.

Approach to Spirituality: In the course of its development, each community will probably add to the common exercises some particular devotions or practices that express a local spirituality. There may be a canon of writings that embody this approach and so are recommended reading during the time of formation. Whatever form it takes, and however it is transmitted, it is important that members of a community share a spirituality that is somehow embedded, embodied, and celebrated in the lifestyle. Otherwise they are merely cohabiting.

Idiom: The community may develop its own argot as a means of expressing insider-status;[27] thus *refectory* is used instead of the

27. On this dynamic in a work environment, see J. A. C. Brown, *The Social Psychology of Industry: Human Relations in the Factory* (Harmondsworth: Pelican, 1954), 146–47.

more usual *dining room,* and various elements of the lifestyle are referenced by terms unfamiliar and mysterious to those outside the group.[28] Monasteries with large properties often designate particular areas by arcane names, handed down through the generations, but baffling to strangers. Such usage is code for belonging.

Rituals: Following the insight of Emile Durkheim (1858–1917), rituals create a sense of identity and belonging that facilitates the acceptance of socially sanctioned beliefs and values. Here we are not limiting ourselves to religious rituals; the normal courtesies of civilized society play a similar role. Values are embedded in rituals and are more easily absorbed. To acknowledge another person on meeting indicates the giving of respect and may induce such an attitude. Of course, the possibility of mere play-acting is never far distant. The role of ritual in community life goes far beyond standard religious ritual as instanced in the liturgy. It includes all the minor ways in which a community expresses itself: the wearing of distinctive clothing, the singing of particular songs, the observance of certain festivities. Think not only of monastic communities, but also of football teams and their supporters.

Relationships: Even the most informal groups have expectations about how members relate to one another, what forms of address they use, and, in some languages, whether intimate pronouns are permitted. It is a very rare group indeed that does not have some form of hierarchy, though it may be implicit and concealed. In some cultures, a particular form of speech is used in addressing oneself to superiors. Even in the most egalitarian group, talents are recognized and utilized even though no titles are conferred. We may be equal in the sight of God and as persons, but when it comes to the exercise of particular competencies, human community functions best when it is the collaboration of unequals.

Boundaries: Most groups have limits, invisible lines often unseen by outsiders and newcomers, beyond which behavior is

---

28. A certain community of religious women is reported to have had the custom of referring to a man as a "piano."

unacceptable. These social norms may exclude particular actions and attitudes that are condoned outside the group. Observing such restrictions is seen as an indication that a person has been socialized and has assumed the group identity. Sometimes these boundaries take the form of enclosure, drawing a clear line between "inside" and "outside," and between those involved in the running of the community and those who opt for a liminal existence.[29]

This determined drawing together of different traditions produces an enriched outcome. It is to be hoped that no one who enters monastic life remains the same. One would hope for a certain growth in refinement,[30] not in the sense of more sophisticated manners but as a more refined sensibility toward others and an increased delicacy in dealing with differences. This comes about only through moving outside one's cultural boundaries and learning to delight in exploring other aspects of human experience. "Culture is born out of exchanges and thrives on differences. In this sense 'national culture' is a self-contradiction and 'multiculturalism' is a pleonasm. The death of culture lies in self-centeredness, self-sufficiency and isolation."[31]

For this desirable fusion to happen there needs to be a certain reserve in asserting one's own culture and a shared willingness to stand back to allow others to express themselves. This restraint is especially necessary on the part of those who hold power in the community—whether their dominance is institutional or informal. We will have more to say about this desirable attitude later. A successful fusion of cultures is witnessed by a shared sense of naturalness and relaxation, in which nobody in the community feels morally compelled to play a role that has to be learned.

29. Diarmuid O'Murchu discusses the connection between liminality and *communitas* in *Reframing Religious Life: An Expanded Vision for the Future* (Slough, UK: St Pauls, 1995), 55.

30. This recalls the title of a book on religious life by Sister Madeleine, OSA, *Solitary Refinement* (London: SCM Press, 1972.)

31. Thus Pierre Ryckmans, quoted by Julian Barnes in *The London Review of Books*, 20 April 2017, 43.

Negotiating differences is a lifelong challenge for all who aspire to live in community—as it is in marriages. We who desire to be of one heart and one mind often find it difficult to see why others seem to view matters differently, and to act out of different values. Even when we are convinced that our way of assessing the situation is the correct one—and this is usually our belief—we have to learn how, as Saint Augustine wrote, "to hate the sin but love the sinner." To arrive at such a desirable state, we have to get into the habit of not wanting to re-create others in our own likeness but, rather, to seek to be content to allow others to be what they are, to rejoice because they are different from us.

The key to this desirable process of mutual enrichment is integral listening, encouraging others to express what they are and welcoming what is thus manifested. The art of listening, however, is not something that is acquired cheaply. It demands a high level of renunciation. For one thing, we have to stop speaking; it is impossible to speak and listen simultaneously. To some extent we have to stop thinking—calculating, responding, and crafting an answer mean utilizing a different part of the brain; for the time being, we have to blank out and be receptive. Often we have to dismantle our prejudices that prevent us from hearing the clear message that the words embody. Often we have to step away from the formation we have received as members of a family and a culture and be prepared to see matters from a different perspective.

As we will see, the monastic virtue of authentic humility has a real contribution to make in equipping us for dialogue with others and for the willingness to allow things to be done in ways different from what our own culture would expect. And this not only builds good community; it also increases our own measure of happiness.

6

Neither Slaves nor Children

In the paranetic sections of the Epistle to the Ephesians and the Epistle to the Colossians, children are instructed to obey (*hupak-ouete*) their parents (Eph 6:1; Col 3:20), and slaves are instructed to obey their masters (Eph 6:5; Col 3:22). Wives are not instructed to obey their husbands but only to be subordinate (*hypotassesthe*) to them (Col 3:18; Titus 2:5; 1 Pet 3:1; 3:5). The injunction in Eph 5:21 is more general: "Be subordinate to each other [or one another] in the fear of [or reverence for] Christ." Since the whole section concerns husbands and wives, it seems likelier that the spouses are being exhorted to practice mutual subordination, giving way to each other rather than asserting their preferences. Inevitably the form of such subordination would be a matter of conforming to the existing order. In a world in which vertical social order was paramount, acting according to one's standing in that order was regarded as an essential means of maintaining social harmony. In a patriarchal society, this meant that women were expected to keep their secondary place, even though there were probably many subtle ways of subverting the system. To act otherwise was to be seen as insubordinate or disorderly, out of order. We may not agree with this ancient view of human hierarchy, but the point is that this subordination was less constricting than complete servitude.[1] Total submission was expected of slaves and children; they had no status and were considered to have no rights; they were incapable of acting independently; they were "under guardians" (Gal 4:2). What was expected of children and slaves was that they would do what they were told; they were not considered to have any worthwhile contribution to make in deciding what should be done. They were subject to arbitrary violence without redress or recourse to a higher tribunal. If they acted contrary to their master's wishes they were flogged.

This preliminary consideration leads us to the point that when we speak of the function of "obedience" in the monastic community we have to be careful that we are not led astray by considerations based on the beliefs and values of the ancient world, still prevalent in parts of today's secular society. It is an abuse of authority to reduce monks and nuns to the level of slaves or children, obliged to do what they are told without being involved in the process of decision-making. Even though Saint Benedict shows some signs of interpreting obedience in an absolutist sense, especially in the chapters borrowed from the Rule of the Master, the authority of the abbot in the Rule is not untrammeled. It is subject to several constraints.[2] And it seems that Saint Benedict's position on obedience shifts in the course of the Rule from an austere echoing and even a certain strengthening of his source in chapter 5, to a more humane vision as the Rule nears its end. Tyranny (RB 27.6) remains tyranny even if it practiced sweetly under the relatively benign disguise of paternalism or maternalism.

---

1. In several Asian countries, especially those influenced by traditional Confucian or Islamic ideals, men were customarily seen as inherently superior. It was expected that women would be obedient to their fathers and brothers when young, then to their husbands, and later even to their male progeny. Needless to say, this traditional notion is widely challenged today, at least in the West.

2. See Michael Casey and David Tomlins, *Introducing Benedict's Rule: A Program of Formation* (Sankt Ottilien: Eos Verlag, 2006), 49–53. The six restraints discussed there are fidelity to the Rule, free community election, due process, threat of deposition, the prospect of hell, and community inertia.

Especially in the West, the Church has given priority to what may be termed an "ideology of obedience," according to which the Church is a rigidly hierarchical structure in which the primary duty of each member is to render unquestioning obedience to those higher up.[3] That this approach has led to serious issues and some real stupidity is clear. Dysmas de Lassus, the Prior General of the Carthusians, has drawn attention to spiritual abuse in religious life, a problem he regards as related to and not less serious than sexual abuse, which, after all, is often more about power than the gratification of lust.[4] The danger is greater in new foundations or in newly reformed communities where the role of the superior is more prominent (102). Abuse occurs when there is no clear distinction between the superior and the rule (110) and there is an absolute identity between the will/whim of a superior and the will of God (164ff). Not so long ago, a certain abbot reminded by his prior that a particular decision was contrary to the rule replied, in the manner of Louis XIV and Charles de Gaulle, "La règle? C'est moi." Usually superiors caught in this trap are supported by loyal lieutenants who do much of the dirty work for them, so that their hands remain unsullied. "At the head of these communities are often seen two or three confidants, brothers or sisters, around the superior, like an inner circle. These act as the superior's eyes and ears."[5] These can often be recognized because they have privileged access to the resources of the community not available to those farther from the center. Many years ago a psychologist who often worked with groups of habited religious told me that he could always identify

---

3. In contrast, Saint Augustine makes the point that the keys delivered to Peter were given not to him alone but to all who belong to the unity of the Church: *tibi trado, quod omnibus traditum est* (*Sermo* 295; PL 38:1349).

4. Dysmas de Lassus, *Risques et dérives de la vie religieuse* (Paris: Cerf, 2020). He writes, "The high value placed on obedience in the religious life makes it especially vulnerable to a form of spiritual abuse that is less visible and more difficult to grasp" (24).

5. Lassus, *Risques et dérives*, 64.

this inner circle because of their more expensive spectacles, watches, and shoes. Today the giveaway would be their more elaborate cell phones. Closeness to power usually brings tangible privileges.

To be called to exercise authority in a monastic community ideally means restrictions placed on personal derogation from the common life.[6] "The more he is promoted above the rest, so much the more should he be diligent in observing the precepts of the rule" (RB 65.17). Abbatial exceptionalism not only reduces the abbot's credibility as a guide to monastic living but also opens the way to more serious abuses. The problem is compounded when the mandate is indefinitely prolonged. In some cases, the call to serve as abbot is thought to effect some kind of ontological trans-formation, so that even when the mandate is complete, at least some of the privileges remain, along with the honorific titles and the jewelry. Perhaps forgetful of RB 2.39, some abbots are buried with all their baubles of rank, perhaps in the hope of special treat-ment at the Judgment.

It needs to be said that giving a command "in virtue of holy obedience" is even more demanding than responding to such an injunction. It not only means scrutinizing personal motivations to ensure purity of intention, but also demands that the superior discern the condition of the other person so that what is enjoined may truly be life-giving for the one commanded and not just a pleasurable exercise in domination.

For the obedience rendered in a monastic context to be virtuous it must be given by free adults, not by children or by slaves. Real obedience occurs only when there is the option of not obeying.[7]

---

6. Lassus quotes the Carthusian Statutes (26.8): "The procurator and the other officials of the house will take care not to abuse their office in granting to them-selves superfluities that they would not permit to others" (*Risques et dérives*, 111). William of Malmsbury, writing of the first Cistercians, affirmed that their abbots permitted nothing to themselves that was not permitted to others: *Abbas nihil sibi nisi quod aliis licere permittit (Gesta Regum Anglorum* §336; PL 179:1289).

7. Lassus (186) quotes this sentiment from an article by M.-M. Labourdette, OP, *Cours de théologie morale*, t. II. (Paris: *Parole et Silence*, 2012), 57.

We might well consider the sentiment voiced by Dorothy Day: "The paradox of obedience is that it cannot be asked of someone else; it can only be voluntarily given by oneself."[8]

This was certainly the case in those who came to seek counsel from the Desert Fathers; they looked for one who had wisdom rather than one who had jurisdiction. In deliberately choosing the source of advice, according to the famous *dictum* of Jean-Paul Sartre, they effectively chose their own future direction by their choice of director. The same is probably true of the obedience given today to a spiritual director. It is given, not imposed. This ties in with a thought that was expressed at the 2012 Abbots' Congress by Cardinal Braz de Aviz: "He who commands must command as a brother, and he who obeys must obey as a brother." The freedom envisaged here—to use the distinction made by Jacques Maritain— is not freedom from obligation, but rather freedom from coercion, in whatever form this is exercised. Maritain quotes with approval a sentence from Yves Simon: "The progress of liberty implies the substitution of persuasion for coercion wherever this substitution can be reasonably realized."[9] Good abbots are convincing persuaders. Coercion remains coercion even when it does not invoke

---

8. I am not sure whether this is a direct quotation or a paraphrase. It is taken from Kate Hennessy, *Dorothy Day: The World will be Saved by Beauty: An Intimate Portrait of My Grandmother* (New York: Scribner, 2017), 258.

9. In this connection Maritain writes, "1) It is inherent in the very notion of a community of human persons that such a community involves a division *du travail*, a differentiation or specialization of the parts of this whole as regards the proper working or functioning of each one of them. 2) It is inherent in the notion of such a differentiation or specialization that some parts of this whole have as their *proper* working, as their *special* functioning, the care of the *whole* itself and of its common good. Such is, in my opinion, the reason for which even in a community made up of perfectly intelligent, well-informed and virtuous men an authority must exist, directed toward the common good of the whole. Internal improvements of the intellect and will, special habitus and special virtues must develop in some parts in order to keep at its best that special function which bears upon the whole as such" (Jacques Maritain, "On Authority," *The Review of Politics* 3, no. 2 (April 1941): 250–54. Accessed 25 July 2018 from https://maritain.nd.edu/jmc/jm-ys.htm.

external sanctions; it is easy to invade another's rightful liberty by moral pressure and the unspoken threat of displeasure, disapproval, and rejection.

 The primary task of the community and of those to whom its governance is entrusted is to lead the members of the community toward that fulfillment intended by God in their creation and vocation. I have already quoted Notker Wolf on this matter: "The purpose of real authority is to help people to become independent and discover what lies within their capabilities: in other words, help them to become free."[10] This freedom is the incredible lightness of being that is experienced by those who find themselves in exactly the situation God intended in creating them. This is what Dom Hubert van Zeller meant when he suggested that true freedom is "the ability to be true to God's idea of me—that is to myself and to my vocation."[11]

There is a huge task of discernment imposed on those who wield authority in a monastic community. As Saint Benedict says, "Let [the abbot] know how difficult and demanding is the task he has received, to govern souls and to be at the service of many [different] characters (*multorum servire moribus*)" (RB 2.31). The point to be emphasized is that, in a Benedictine community, authority is person-centered rather than task-centered. Superiors have to adapt themselves to those in their care, not vice versa. An abbot who, to all intents and purposes, uses his office to implement his personal vision and to impose his preferences on the community will quickly lose credibility as a spiritual guide. He retains jurisdiction, but, in any real sense, his *auctoritas* has been seriously diminished.

Saint Benedict characterizes the three tasks of the abbot by the following verbs: *docere, constituere, iubere.* He is to teach, to

10. Notker Wolf and Enrica Rosanna, *The Art of Leadership* (Collegeville, MN: Liturgical Press, 2013), 5.

11. Hubert van Zeller, *The Holy Rule: Notes on St. Benedict's Legislation for Monks* (London: Sheed and Ward, 1959), 5.

establish as policy, and to give commands. Ideally there is harmony between these elements of his ministry and, more, even a certain continuity flowing from doctrine to policy to practical administration. His fundamental task is at the level of beliefs and values. He is to sprinkle the yeast of his doctrine in the minds of the disciples (RB 2.5). The image of yeast is significant. Yeast does not replace the dough or overwhelm it—yeast gives a certain dynamic lightness that transforms and enhances that which receives it. The role of teaching is central to Saint Benedict's view of authority, and, as we shall discuss later, the reception of abbatial teaching is the heart of what he understands as "obedience."

The Benedictine abbot is not a professor of theology. His teaching is concrete. His task is to bring the Gospel message to bear on the daily lives of the monks. Done consistently over a protracted period, and in a way that builds consensus in the community, abbatial teaching leads to a body of beliefs and values that implicitly or explicitly forms the basis for a community policy. The effect of this is that, for the most part, the community can run on automatic pilot. Beyond the appointment of officials, there are adjustments to be made from time to time, and, occasionally, there will be emergencies to which a rapid response must be made. These are dealt with by the abbot's authority to issue commands. In general, a monastic community can be expected to operate smoothly without the constant issuing of a plethora of particular instructions. Micro-management from on high is an insult to the *humanitas* of the community.

Another way of describing the abbatial task is to say that it is a matter of formation of conscience. "The education of the conscience guarantees freedom and engenders peace of heart."[12] Those who have been socialized in the contemporary secular world will probably need to undergo some kind of detoxifying process if they are to live under the guidance of the Gospel. Their attitude to telling

12. *Catechism of the Catholic Church*, §1784.

the truth, for example, will almost certainly need upgrading.[13] Those who have made their own the saying, "If it feels good, do it," will need to learn to distinguish emotion from reasonableness in choosing a course of action. And all of us have to be educated in discerning God's will, in separating the tangled web of our own inner volitions from the authentic inspirations of the Holy Spirit. There is a lifetime's work here, and part of the abbot's role is to facilitate its progress by teaching and policy and directives.

This task becomes particularly challenging in those cultures that place a high value on social conformity, deference to elders, and adherence to accepted norms, even when these are unformulated.[14] A generalized implementation of such attitudes leads to a peaceful, harmonious, and well-ordered community. At least superficially. Underneath the surface, volcanoes may be stirring toward a point of eruption. Although it is true that, to some extent, external practice can facilitate the development of the corresponding interior values, there is a danger that a merely external formation will leave untouched the inner principles that govern personal choices. A person may feel shame when exposed as being in some way deviant, but this does not necessarily lead to an inner conversion, just the stricter observance of the eleventh commandment: "Thou shalt not get caught." Shame can be effective as a means of social control, but it does little to re-orient a person's basic philosophy.[15]

13. See Michael Casey, *The Art of Winning Souls: Pastoral Care of Novices* (Collegeville, MN: Liturgical Press, 2012), 72–74.

14. The Japanese word of the year for 2017 was the term *Sontaku*; this refers to a preemptive sycophancy by which an inferior or employee may act reprehensively in order to conform to the unspoken wishes of a superior, even to the point of allowing themselves to accept full responsibility for any crimes committed in the name of the superior and for his benefit.

15. For a wide-ranging discussion and critique of the role of shame in enforcing conformity, see Martha C. Nussbaum, *Hiding from Humanity: Disgust, Shame, and the Law* (Princeton: Princeton University Press, 2004), 337: "Shame, in particular, does come in less problematic and more admirable forms, but it is so hard to distinguish these forms from the bad forms, and so common to find a slippage from one to another, that the prominent use of shame in punishment

Whereas guilt is focused on one's actions (which can be upgraded), shame is directed toward one's very being. Shaming undermines self-respect and, instead of contributing toward an integrated and more harmonious society, has the effect of pushing its target into an underclass marked by isolation and rejection.[16]

The purpose of the formation given by the abbot is to create an ordered community that is, to a large extent, self-sustaining. Living in a world marked by social chaos, Benedict saw the monastery as an island of good order surrounded by a wild sea of disturbance.[17] Many communities inscribe the word *pax* above their doorways, indicating that peacefulness is the specific characteristic of a functional Benedictine community. And, according to the well-known axiom of Saint Augustine, "The peace of all things is the tranquility of order." He continues, "Order is the organization of like and unlike things, giving to each its place."[18] The Benedictine monastery is a haven of peace because it is well-organized. It is a stable community that operates within a network of beliefs and values, expressed concretely in a Rule, moderated by an abbot elected by the community, who is skilled in discernment (RB 64.17-19) and able to bring forth from his wealth of wisdom "new things and old" (RB 64.9).[19]

---

and lawmaking seems tantamount to inviting people to discriminate and stigmatize."

16. Saint Benedict uses shame (*verecundia*) as a means of compelling punctuality in his monks (RB 43.7), and similar provisions, such as excommunication and public exclusion from the sacraments, can be found in the ecclesiastical armory of sanctions. Punishments that are vindictive rather than remedial habitually generate little positive benefit.

17. See Michael Casey, "Saint Benedict's View of Order," *Tjurunga* 72 (2007): 30–45.

18. Saint Augustine, *De civitate Dei* 19:13; CC 48:679.

19. I have tried to sketch out how the role of an abbot as teacher might be brought into current practice in "Monasticism: Present and Future: Part II," ABR 65, no. 3 (September 2014), especially 300–305. Regarding teachers, Saint Gregory the Great insists on the importance of avoiding arrogance: *Moralia in Iob* 23.23–24; CC 143B:1161–62.

The way that Saint Benedict envisages the daily regimen requires the abbot to take a largely non-interventionist role. The two major daily activities, sleeping and the celebration of the *Opus Dei*, are largely self-regulating. Several hours are devoted to personal *lectio divina*. The area in which a command structure might be thought to operate was daily manual work. Here subsidiarity seems to have been the norm. Formation, reception of guests, and care of the sick were farmed out to responsible individuals, each operating in a zone separate from the community. Craftsmen were to carry out their trade under a general mandate from the abbot (RB 57.1). The rest was left to the immediate attention of the cellarer, the deans, and the prior—all operating in accordance with abbatial policy. The aim seems to have been to create a smoothly running organization that did not require constant abbatial interventions. The abbot, however, has to have a care for giving the signal for the *Opus Dei* unless he can find someone responsible to act as bell-ringer (RB 47.1). This seems to indicate that the abbot is to exercise a practical oversight of the smooth running of the monastic day, rather than to be continually interfering with it by repeated commands. Such a monastery would have succeeded in arriving at a creative monotony, an unexciting external life that would provide ample scope for interior and spiritual activity.[20] Benedict made provision for a more placid monasticism[21] than was envisaged in the *Rule of the Master*, perhaps sometimes subordinating external efficiency to the overriding priority of pursuing the one thing necessary, seeking God.

Let me describe an example of the exact opposite of what Saint Benedict was hoping to achieve. In one monastery of my acquain-

---

20. See Michael Casey, "An Unexciting Life: The Sober Spirituality of Saint Benedict," in *An Unexciting Life: Reflections on Benedictine Spirituality* (Petersham, MA: St. Bede's Publications, 2005), 13–26. The title was inspired by a quotation from a letter of Gustave Flaubert, "Be regular and ordinary in your life, like a bourgeois, so that you may be violent and original in your work."

21. May Saints Maur and Placid forgive the pun.

tance, the now-deceased foundress filled all the important offices in the community in addition to her own. She was effectively cellarer, chantress, formator, infirmarian, and electrician, and she also concerned herself with any guests who seemed worthy of cultivation. When pressed by the visitator to appoint others to these posts, she nominated persons who would hold the title but be completely subservient to her, so that nothing was changed. Admittedly there was a high level of efficiency in the community because of the concentration of power, but something was lost. This became clear after she was compelled to resign—it was very hard to find anyone with the confidence and the necessary skills to succeed her in any of the variety of tasks she had assumed.

Here it has to be remarked that obedience in the typical Benedictine monastery up to the Middle Ages and beyond was concerned mainly with the internal regimen of the monastery. With the rise of apostolic religious life and the changes brought to the activities undertaken by Benedictine communities—notably due to the restrictions imposed by Austro-Hungarian Emperor Joseph II on "useless" religious orders and, elsewhere, the expansion of missionary Benedictinism in the nineteenth century—obedience came to be more concerned with the ordering of external activities and, particularly, the assignment of individuals to particular apostolates. In this context, the monastic understanding of the vow of obedience as being almost identical to that of *conversatio morum* almost disappeared. Instead of being a commitment to live according to the ever-changing demands of monastic life, it became an element in a vertical command structure. The typical moment of obedience was seen to be the willing acceptance of an order and its prompt implementation. This was a guarantee of an efficient structure of governance that would moderate and control the works of the apostolate, but it was not quite what Saint Benedict envisaged, especially in his later years.

Monasteries with long histories have to deal with tangled webs of influence on the way they embody the ideals of monastic living. There are many conflicting claims to balance: the Rule itself, the

Constitutions, the immemorial customs of the house, the needs and aspirations of the members of the community, the demands of income-generating activities and apostolates, social and ecclesiastical expectations, historical precedents, and so many other modifiers of the monastic ideal taken in the abstract.

This is where the initial conference of John Cassian demonstrates its usefulness. There is a need for some fundamental discernment of the goal for which people enter monasteries and a search to formulate objectives whereby this goal may be realized. It is by no means certain that those entering today are seeking the same life-forms as those who entered generations ago. While respecting the choices that have been prudently made in the past, it is probably worthwhile asking whether some change of direction is appropriate to service the aspirations of the younger generation—especially when they are looking for a "monastic" alternative to working in parishes or educational institutions. For communities whose days have been filled with ministry, it may well be difficult to find tasks to occupy the monks every day of the year. There is only so much sweeping and dusting that needs doing.

As to the way in which authority is exercised in a community whose energies are deployed in several different directions, I would suggest that, as many communities have found, the solution may lie in a contemporary rereading of the twentieth chapter of the Rule, where Saint Benedict speaks about dividing the administration of the monastery into deaneries. In this way governance of the different activities of the monastery can be delegated to trustworthy members of the community, while the superior's solicitude is more pastoral, concentrating on maintaining contact with all the members of the community, generating a solid level of teaching in the community, establishing consensual policy, and, with the aid of a council, exercising a supervisory role over the different departments. By law the superior cannot compel religious to manifest their conscience. This means that if there is to be access to interior data, in order to be more responsive to the spiritual needs of the community, a superior must endeavor to win a high level of trust. A Benedictine superior is not obliged to be a micro-manager.[22]

In contrast to the assertion of Marilyn Dunn that "throughout the bulk of the rule, Benedict's view of community relations emerges as a predominantly vertical one,"[23] Adalbert de Vogüé notes a certain horizontalism in the later chapters of the Rule. As we have already noted,

> Every member of the community, by virtue of his age and seniority, plays a part in the educative role which in traditional coenobitism was reserved to the abbot and to the office-holders. The chapter "On Good Zeal" attributes even more generously to the life of charitable fraternal relationships, the purifying and sanctifying effects which the Master saw as the result of asceticism lived under the abbot's direction."[24]

22. We find a late-nineteenth-century echo of this style of leadership in the Australian foundress Saint Mary of the Cross: "Mary MacKillop does not use the term 'authority' as much as one might have expected. A Superior to her is not an authority figure, that is, not someone who is there to enforce obedience. She is there to guide the Sisters under her care and to have the gentleness of the Sacred Heart" (Margaret Paton, *Mary MacKillop: The Ground of Her Loving* (London: Darton, Longman & Todd, 2010), 104.

23. Marilyn Dunn, *The Emergence of Monasticism: From the Desert Fathers to the Early Middle Ages* (Oxford: Blackwell, 2003), 120. It may be remarked that Dunn's rejection of the dependence of Benedict's Rule on that of the Master leads to a weakness in appreciating the redactional history of the text. For much of Benedict's lifetime his rule was a work in progress.

24. Adalbert de Vogüé, *Community and Abbot in the Rule of Saint Benedict*, CS 5/2 (Kalamazoo, MI: Cistercian Publications, 1988), 430–31. We can generate some data on horizontal relationships by noting that in RB the community is a fraternity based on honor, respect, gratitude (4.8, 70; 63; 72.4). This is expressed by listening (3.2-3; 4.55; 61.4) and is reinforced by service (35.1-2; 57.7; Basil, *Long Rules* 7). Common life is assured by structures (3.7), celebrated in ritual (35.15-18; 44; 58; 67.3-4). Discord is repaired by forgiveness (4.73; 27.1-9). Stability gives birth to a sense of belonging (58.26; 63) and creates a

It is true that "With the Master we re-enter into the Egyptian stream, transmitted to the West by Cassian, whereby the authority of the superior takes first place as the fundamental principle of the community."[25] But with the passage of the years this perspective was nuanced by Saint Benedict to provide more scope for delegated officials: prior, deans, formator, infirmarian, and guestmaster, and to give greater responsibility to the seniors for maintaining the quality of the *conversatio*. The ideal of mutual obedience is also proposed, even though the provisions he makes are far from exploiting the full potential of such a proposal.[26] And he allows the possibility of appeal against commands that seem impossible. And Benedict recommends that the abbot take all decisions with counsel, even in those matters that are relatively unimportant, even to the extent of paying attention to the feedback given by visiting monks. This is far from exercising a tyranny over the strong while maintaining the singular authority of the abbot. It is, in practice, a very collegial form of governance, that is both more effective and less stressful for both superior and community.

It is perhaps significant that Sandra Schneiders speaks about this kind of governance as important for the flourishing of religious life in the twenty-first century:

---

climate of trust and mutuality (69; 70; 71), while it also facilitates generativity (21.1-4; 31.1-2; 57.1; 58.6).

25. Adalbert de Vogüé, "Le monastère, Église du Christ," in *Commentationes in Regulam S. Benedicti,* ed. Basilius Steidle, Studia Anselmiana 42 (Rome: Herder, 1957), 33.

26. "From the very beginning of the chapter, Benedict seems nervous. He sets out to discuss mutual obedience, but he is well aware that the dominant form of obedience is hierarchical. Therefore he is very careful to cover his flanks by disclaimers. Unfortunately, this preoccupation with rank will take him completely off the track of his subject and eventually lead him to exaggerated claims for hierarchical obedience in 71.6–9" (Terrence G. Kardong, *Benedict's Rule: A Commentary* [Collegeville, MN: Liturgical Press, 1996], 582). Later (p. 586), he says of RB 71, "It does not take account of community life in any realistic sense. No system that requires underlings to solve all conflict by capitulation and self-accusation can be said to be healthy."

Many in the hierarchy are still operating within a premodern model of society, that is of the church as a divine right monarchy in which authority flows in one direction only, namely downward, and can be exercised absolutely on the assumption that the subordinates have no rights except those bestowed upon them by the superiors.

Religious in general are operating within a different model, one that has developed over the past two centuries in non-totalitarian societies and that was, in principle, enshrined in the documents of Vatican II in its recognition of the rights of the baptized in their church and the inviolable freedom of conscience. This equality and freedom are the basis for a theology of obedience as an exercise in asymmetrical mutuality rather than abject subordination.

And:

Religious life is intrinsically, that is, by its very nature, a voluntary, egalitarian network of Gospel-based relationships in which power is not exercised hierarchically and therefore cannot normally be exercised coercively.

And:

[Contemporary Religious Life], especially among women in the first world and increasingly in the developing world, is deeply egalitarian. This is not a political option for a democratic form of government (which is hardly egalitarian!) but a theological and spiritual option for the kind of non-hierarchical community Jesus founded and for its collegial rather than monarchical structure and function.[27]

Reconsidering the functioning of authority and obedience in our communities may well be one of the more important ways

---

27. Sandra Schneiders, *Buying the Field: Catholic Religious Life in Mission to the World* (New York: Paulist Press, 2013), 547, 456, 505.

that we can fulfill the double mandate of the Vatican Council: to return to our sources and to be attentive to the signs of our times. In this, many of us may be surprised to find some good indications in a number of recent documents from the Vatican's Congregation for Institutes of Consecrated Life and Societies of Apostolic Life (CICLSAL). I refer to two in particular, both obtainable from the Vatican's website: *Faciem tuam, Domine, requiram* (The Service of Authority and Obedience) of 11 May 2008, and *New Wine in New Wineskins: The Consecrated Life and its Ongoing Challenges since Vatican II* of 6 January 2017.[28]

The problems of spiritual abuse in religious life that prompted Dysmas de Lassus to write his book *Risques et dérives de la vie religieuse* are clearly visible in these texts.[29] Although some may

28. As with most documents produced by a group, these texts could be improved by radical editing to eliminate padding, duplication, alien idiom due to translation, unresolved compromises that demand further discussion, and window-dressing inserted to placate imagined critics. Perhaps the objective of the documents needs to be pursued explicitly with greater singleness of purpose. The content is good, but its delivery needs to be crisper. Without this, reading them is hard work. The laudable effort to find gender-inclusive terms sometimes makes the prose awkward. In the future, perhaps two simultaneous versions could be produced, identical except for gender specificity.

29. "The service of authority is not excluded from the current crisis affecting the consecrated life. At first glance, certain situations still show a tendency towards the vertical concentration of the exercising of authority, on both the local and higher levels, thus avoiding the necessary subsidiarity. In some cases, the insistence of some superiors on the personal nature of their authority, almost to the point of thwarting collaboration of the councils, convinced that they are answering (autonomously) to their own conscience, might seem suspect. Consequently, there is a weak or inefficient corresponsibility in government practices, or even the absence of proper authority" (*New Wine*, 19). "In recent years, and especially in recently founded institutes, there have been episodes and situations of manipulation of the freedom and dignity of people. Not only reducing them to a total dependence that mortified their dignity, and sometimes even their fundamental human rights, but sometimes even leading them, with various means of deception and the pretense of loyalty to God's plans through charism, to a form of submission even in the realms of morality and sexual intimacy. With

consider discouragement, inattention, and incompetence to be more serious restraints on abbatial effectiveness,[30] different forms of spiritual abuse exist, though they are not always recognized by those conducting the regular visitations. This omission is often due to the fact that, since the Council, little effort has been made to find a perspective on authority and obedience that corresponds to the reality of our time.[31]

In particular an approach to obedience must be based on respect for the human person: religious are neither slaves nor children.[32] It is not only a question of giving persons their due respect and recognizing their inherent dignity; it is a matter of proactively *promoting* the dignity of each.[33] This involves "paying attention

---

great scandal for all when the facts are brought to light" (*New Wine*, 20). See also Pavel Syssoev, *De la paternité spirituelle et de ses contrafaçons* (Paris: Cerf, 2020).

30. The document recognizes and even insists on the difficulty of the service of authority and warns against the possibility of discouragement and disillusionment leading to inertia: "What we see here then is the danger of becoming managers of the routine, resigned to mediocrity, restrained from intervening, no longer having the courage to point out the purposes of authentic consecrated life and running the risk of losing the love of one's first fervour and the desire to witness to it" (*Faciem,* §28).

31. "At this point, more than fifty years after the closing of the Council, the permanence of government styles and practices that . . . move away from or contradict the spirit of service, to the point of degenerating into forms of authoritarianism, cannot but worry us all" (*New Wine*, 43).

32. "The culture of Western Society, strongly centred on the subject, has contributed to the spread of the value of respect for the dignity of the human person, positively fostering the person's free development and autonomy. Such recognition constitutes one of the most significant traits of modernity and is a providential given which requires new ways of conceiving authority and relating to it" (*Faciem*, §2).

33. "*Persons in authority are called to promote the dignity of the person*, paying attention to each member of the community and to his or her growth, giving to each one the appropriate appreciation and positive consideration, nurturing sincere affection towards all and keeping reserved all that is said in confidence. It is appropriate to recall that before invoking obedience (necessary),

to the normal growth of each one in every phase and season of life, in order to guarantee that 'youthfulness of spirit which lasts through time.' "[34] There is a strong subtext throughout the documents indicated by some elements of style. The term "persons in authority" is preferred to "Superiors";[35] "brothers/sisters" is preferred to "sons/daughters."[36] This is more than a trivial change. The documents take seriously the primacy of communion and, thence, of "fraternity" in religious communities.[37] Furthermore, in this context, the identification of the office of superior with an individual, so that one person holds office beyond what is useful, leads to many aberrations.[38]

Throughout the documents there is a recognition that the task of exercising authority in religious life is very difficult, especially

---

one needs to practice charity (indispensable)" (*Faciem,* § 13c). "In certain cases infantile subjection and scrupulous dependence are promoted instead of collaboration 'with an active and responsible obedience.' This can betray the dignity of a person to the point of humiliation" (*New Wine*, 25).

34. *Faciem,* §13g.

35. "In the context in which we live, even the terminology *superiors* and *subjects* is no longer suitable. What worked in a pyramidal and authoritative relational context is no longer desirable or livable in the sensitivity of communion of our way [of] feeling like and wanting to be a Church" (*New Wine*, 24).

36. "There is a common impression that the evangelical foundation of fraternity is sometimes missing in the relationship between superiors and subjects. More importance is given to the institution than to the people it is made up of" (*New Wine*, 24).

37. "In the broader view of consecrated life since the Council, we have passed from the centrality of the role of authority to the centrality of the dynamic of fraternity. For this reason, authority must be at the service of communion; a true ministry to accompany brothers and sisters towards conscious and responsible fidelity" (*New Wine*, 41). With the publication of *Fratelli tutti* on October 6, 2020, Pope Francis has insisted on the importance (and inclusivity) of the notion of fraternity.

38. " 'Superiors, constituted for a definite time, do not remain too long in offices of governance without interruption' [*CIC*, c. 624, §2]. This norm of Canon Law is still in the reception process; there are considerable variables in institutional practices" (*New Wine*, 46).

because it involves setting aside personal preferences and priorities and listening with great attention to all the members of the community, not just to a favored few. In particular, attention needs to be devoted to ensuring that the style of governance reflects attitudes different from those of the past and those found in military circles and business corporations. In the first place privileges and perquisites are to be kept at a minimum, and exceptions to the common rule limited to those necessary for the exercise of the ministry of service.[39] Peremptory commands and bureaucratic manipulation are to give way to a more humane and friendly relationship, in which the members of a community are left in no doubt that what is asked of them is truly God's will, and not merely authoritarian whimsy.[40] The requirement of explicit permissions should not be multiplied but be reserved for what is truly necessary.[41]

What all this means is that a lot of the baggage hitherto associated with religious obedience needs to be discarded. Both theory and practice need diligent re-examination. The responsibility for

39. "The distribution of goods in communities must always be done with respect for justice and corresponsibility. . . . We cannot accept a management style in which the economic autonomy of a few corresponds to the dependence of others, thereby undermining the sense of reciprocal belonging and the guarantee of fairness, even in the recognition of differences of role and service" (*New Wine*, 27).

40. "Persons in authority must act in such a way that the brothers or the sisters can perceive that when they give a command, they are doing so only to obey God. . . . [T]hose in authority, on their part, must search assiduously with the help of prayer, reflection, and the advice of others for what God really wills. Otherwise, instead of representing God, superiors risk putting themselves carelessly in God's place" (*Faciem*, §12).

41. "In the day-to-day service of authority, people should not be made to constantly ask permission to carry out normal day-to-day operations. Those who exercise power should not encourage infantile attitudes that can lead to non-responsible behaviours. This path is not likely to lead people to maturity. Unfortunately these kinds of situations are more common than many of us are willing to accept and denounce, and are more evident in women's institutes" (*New Wine*, 21).

this review devolves on those to whom the task of leadership has been given. It is, as the Congregation seems to believe, a task barely begun.

7

Common Work

Many monasteries have embraced the motto *ora et labora,* believing it to be an ancient formula, perhaps tracing back to Saint Benedict. It is carved on lintels, painted on walls, and stamped on monastic products. On December 17, 2018, a Google search for this phrase yielded about three and a half million hits. Among other instances we discover that there is a board game with this motif, *Ora et labora* is displayed at Lego HQ in Denmark, and it has been adopted as a motto by the city of Toledo, Ohio, in the deviant form *laborare est orare.*[1] It has been recently asserted that *"Ora et labora* (prayer and work) are central tenets of the Holy Rule of Saint Benedict."[2]

Nevertheless, some relatively recent work by Soeur Marie-Benoît Meeuws has demonstrated that no earlier form exists than that propagated by Abbot Maurus Wolter in 1880: "Hence that ancient and most distinguished watchword of monks: *Ora et labora.*"[3] On the basis of the evidence that she presented, we are

---

1. " 'To work is to pray' [is] dreadful because of the cynicism, the justification, the contempt which it expresses" (Jacques Ellul, *Prayer and Modern Man* [New York: The Seabury Press, 1970], 15).

2. Linus Mundy, *A Retreat with Benedict and Bernard: Seeking God Alone—Together* (Cincinnati: St. Anthony Messenger Press, 1998), 56.

3. Soeur Marie-Benoît Meeuws, *"Ora et Labora*: devise bénédictine?" *Collectanea Cisterciensia* 54, no. 3 (1992): 193–219, at 213.

led to the conclusion that *Ora et labora* is no more than one of the spurious medievalisms of which the nineteenth century was so fond. It has no real authority; it is simply a catchy phrase. Although its brevity and simplicity are to be applauded, there is a problem. Wherever two nouns are coordinated rather than subordinated, a kind of sibling rivalry emerges. Is work more important than prayer or vice versa? When it is modified to mean "To work is to pray," the use of the phrase seems to be giving priority to work over prayer to the extent that devoting time exclusively to prayer would seem to have become unnecessary.

Even the most abstemious monks eat sometimes, and so they fall under the edict promulgated by Saint Paul and occasionally cited in early monasticism: "One who does not work shall not eat" (2 Thess 3:9). Despite the cartoon image of monks as fat, lazy, and fond of a tipple, a typical monastic temptation, especially today, is to work too much rather than to luxuriate in indolence.[4]

In most monasteries work is the area in which authority and obedience seem to be most visibly operative. Monks are assigned to particular employments and while employed there operate, at least implicitly, under a mandate. Yet in most situations they enjoy—and that is the point to be noted—a certain amount of freedom, with the usual understanding that the details of their employment will be left to their own discretion. I have observed that sometimes monks who seem less lively during the other monastic observances come alive at work. That is probably why it is a great hardship for a monk to be deprived of a satisfying occupation, and the greatest hardship of all is to leave him without any employment. As Abbot Armand-Jean de Rancé of La Trappe remarked, "A monk would not know how to use profitably the time remaining after other duties have been done without having recourse to spending time in manual work. . . . There are fewer

---

4. For a general review of monastic work, see Michael Casey, "Manual Work in the Rule and Beyond," *Tjurunga* 78 (2010): 38–63.

persons than one may think who can give themselves every day to seven or eight hours of reading."[5]

This seems to be a concern in Saint Benedict's chapter on work, as Vogüé notes: "The whole chapter of Benedict is, therefore, remarkably coherent. From beginning to end he advances to a single goal—the elimination of indolence."[6] This consideration also seems to have governed the approach in later centuries. Smaragdus quotes first the *Rule of Paul and Stephen,* "A monk idle in body can never be idle in mind from unclean thoughts," and then Isidore of Seville: "It is through idleness that the lusts and desires arising from harmful thoughts gather strength."[7]

Notwithstanding the importance of work, commentators are convinced that Benedict's horarium gave the priority to *lectio.* Thus Vogüé: "Generally, however, as far as the intentions of Benedict allow us to guess, the arrangements of his horarium seem calculated first of all from the viewpoint of reading."[8] And even though Benedict seems to give twice as much time to work (six to seven hours work, broken in summer, compared with a total of three hours for *lectio divina*), Terrence Kardong concludes, "RB seems to give precedence to *lectio* over manual labour. *Lectio* is always done during 'prime time' (the morning) and never reduced to less than two hours."[9]

5. [Armand-Jean de Rancé,] *La Régle [sic] de saint Benoist nouvellement traduite et éxpliquée selon son véritable esprit* (Paris: François Muguet and George & Louis Josse, 1689), 2:266–309.

6. Adalbert de Vogüé, *La Règle de S. Benoît,* SCh 185 (Paris: Cerf, 1971), 596.

7. Smaragdus of Saint-Mihiel, *Expositio in Regulam Sancti Benedicti 48,* in Corpus Consuetudinum Monasticarum 8:271; *Smaragdus of Saint Mihiel: Commentary on the Rule of Saint Benedict,* trans. David Barry, CS 212 (Kalamazoo, MI: Cistercian Publications, 2008), 432–33. The first text is from PL 66:957A. See also Harry Hagan, "The Rule of Paul and Stephen: A Translation and Commentary," ABR 58, no. 3 (2007): 313–42. The text of Isidore is from *Regula monachorum* 5.1; PL 83:873B.

8. Vogüé, *La Règle de S. Benoît,* SCh 185:600.

9. Terrence Kardong, "A Structural Comparison of *Regula Magistri* 50 and *Regula Benedicti* 48," *Regulae Benedicti Studia* 8/9 (1982): 93–104.

Apart from chapter 48, there are other parts of the Rule that throw some light on the reality of work in Saint Benedict's monastery: RB 66.6-7 (What is inside the enclosure), RB 57 (The Monastery Tradesmen), RB 32 (The Iron Tools and Things), and RB 35 (The Weekly Cooks). Work was not self-chosen but enjoined, because it was necessary for the good of the community (*necessarius*: 48.13) and was judged not to be destructive of the worker's monasticity (57.2-3). Many duties pass from one monk to another by roster (32.3; 35.1; 38.1; 53.17), presupposing competence (38.12). Some tasks were of a higher status than others (7.49, perhaps 2.18), but, concerning this, monks were not to take issue. Work was seen as a way of creating a spirit of solidarity; solitary work (exclusion from the company of others) is imposed on the excommunicated as punishment (25.3).

The governing criteria for the choice of tasks are necessity (48.3) and obedience (48.11). The monks are to "go out" for their work, at least in summertime (48.3); in wintertime they are to "work at their own task which has been enjoined on them" (48.11), as also in Lent (48.14). Sometimes the monks are too far away to return for the Work of God (50.1).

The range of works in which monks are to be occupied will depend on the local situation. Monks do whatever needs to be done in a particular monastery. RB 66 makes provision for all the necessary work areas to be located within the enclosure: the water supply, the mill, the garden, and the various workshops (66.6). Monks work in the garden and the field (7.63). Monks labor "in the kitchen, in the cellar, in the serving room, in the mill or bakery, in the garden" (46.1). Iron tools are used (32.1). RB 57 speaks about those who exercise income-generating crafts. Concerning Benedict's statement that real monks bring in their own harvest, the conditional form of the sentence indicates that this is not the normal situation. Elsewhere Benedict makes provision for increasing the allowance of food (39.6) or drink (40.5) and for advancing the mealtimes if there is heavy work in the fields (41.4).

A reading of the so-called "Plan of St Gall" reveals provision being made for a variety of occupations within the monastery precincts: administration, hospitality, education, care of the sick, food service, cleaning, laundry, liturgical preparation, and manuscript copying. Mostly done by the hundreds of lay workers, there are several industries operating: geese, hens, gardens,[10] the storing, grinding, drying and crushing of grain, a bakery, a brewhouse, horses, and oxen. Workers included fullers, blacksmiths, goldsmiths, turners, shield makers, sword grinders, curriers, saddlers, shoemakers, and shepherds.[11]

A twelfth-century description of the abbey of Clairvaux gives a listing of some of the work done there by the monks: caring for vineyards, harvesting crops, collecting sticks for firewood, grubbing briars, orchards, fish farming, vegetable gardening, milling of grain, sieving of flour, brewing of beer, fulling of cloth, tanning of leather, cooking, washing, caring for grasslands, and haymaking.[12]

Especially in those monasteries located far from human habitation, a tradition of self-sufficiency evolved whereby monasteries became virtual villages. This was still evident in the large establishments of the nineteenth century and persists in memory if not in reality. Meanwhile monks were adding to the necessary arts and crafts of self-support in new fields of activity: cultural, educational, pastoral—especially after the insistence of Austro-Hungarian Emperor Joseph II that only monasteries that were "useful" could continue to exist.

Obviously, the different occupations of monks each have their specific dynamics in the context of monastic living. It is worthwhile, therefore, to attempt to uncover the role that work played in the spiritual lives of the monks. Aquinata Böckmann suggests five areas in which work functions within monastic life:

---

10. Among the items grown are onions, leeks, celery, coriander, dill, poppies, radishes, chard, garlic, shallot, parsley, chervil, lettuces, pepperwort, parsnips, cabbages, and fennel.

11. Walter Horn and Ernest Born, *The Plan of St Gall* (Berkeley: University of California Press, 1979).

12. Pauline Matarasso, *The Cistercian World: Monastic Writings of the Twelfth Century* (London: Penguin, 1993), 287–92.

It provides a livelihood to support the community.

It is a means of asceticism, a part of a disciplined lifestyle.

It provides the possibility for almsgiving to the poor.

It can help the development of a deeper prayerfulness.

Cooperation builds up a sense of solidarity in the community.[13]

These are significant benefits and provide a checklist for assessing the monasticity of particular employments. It has to be admitted, however, that other approaches are also possible.

If we take seriously the admonitions of Qoheleth, then we should strive to find enjoyment even in the most toilsome of tasks. Every employment has its challenges, but, with a positive attitude, these can be regarded as opportunities for personal growth and not just oppressive afflictions. As Friedrich Nietzsche wrote, "That which does not kill us makes us stronger." Dealing with practical difficulties brings out the best in us. It is also, as Saint Benedict seems to indicate in RB 58.7-8, a good indicator of the seriousness of a man's desire to become a monk.

Finding joy in our work is often the result of paying attention to the quality of what we do, rather than rushing to complete it with the minimum of effort and in the minimum of time. The practice of working mindfully is sometimes called "the pursuit of excellence." Now I realize that such a principle can be misinterpreted. Monasteries are full of perfectionists, and part of the struggle we have throughout our life is to recognize the beauty of imperfection, according to the Japanese aesthetic principle *wabi-sabi*. Not being afraid to own that whatever we do is inherently imperfect, impermanent, and incomplete. It is not unknown that some monks suffer from obsessive compulsive disorder, so that they are constantly tyrannized by the superego to do and redo

13. Aquinata Böckmann, "RB 48: Of the Daily Manual Labor," ABR 59, nos. 2–3 (2008): 141–66, 253–90.

everything, striving unhappily to reach an impossible level of perfection.[14] When we refer to the pursuit of excellence, we are not thinking so much of objective perfection but of something subjective—of persons investing themselves fully in what they are doing, applying all their experience, insight, and skill to the task at hand. It may be cooking or sewing or plowing or writing books. In many cases, working well will involve also the renunciation of the false ideal of multitasking. According to the saying of Gregory the Great that has been passed on through the centuries: *Age quod agis.*[15]

Pope Francis has spoken of the danger of efficiency squeezing out the human values in work: "Have the courage to go against the tide of this culture of efficiency, this culture of waste."[16] This is not to undervalue the role of sequential logic in the ordering of tasks but to avoid forcing an unnatural pace with the only purpose being to finish work as soon as possible or to get more things done in the time available.

The quality of work done is to be taken into consideration as well as its quantity. While it is true that measurable goals are more likely to garner attention and be achieved, sometimes less quantifiable goals are more important not only in themselves, but also for the completion of a particular project. What has been called "metric fixation"[17] may lead to the situation in which significant areas of monastic observance are judged to be less amenable to public

14. "This always working to perfect / That which by nature must remain imperfect" (Geoffrey Hill, *Broken Hierarchies: Poems 1952–2012* [Oxford: Oxford University Press, 2014]).

15. *Homilies on the Gospel* 37.9; CC 141:355; *Dialogues 4*, 58.1; SCh 265:194.

16. Pope Francis, "Homily at XXVIII World Youth Day: 27 July 2013," in *L'Osservatore Romano* 29–30 July 2013, 4. In an address to the Pontifical Academy of the Social Sciences on 20 October 2017 he said, "We cannot sacrifice on the altar of efficiency—the 'golden calf' of our times—fundamental values such as democracy, justice, freedom, the family, and creation."

17. By Gerry Mueller of the Catholic University of America, interviewed on *Late Night Live* on 14 February 2018.

admiration and, thus, to convey less status, and, as a result, not to be given as much energy as more visible attainments.

One way of understanding the emphasis on the subjective quality of work is to think of it in terms of "flow." In 1990 Mihaly Csikszentmihalyi published his book *Flow: The Psychology of Optimal Experience*, introducing a new term into the language.[18] The optimal experiences about which he wrote were moments in which persons are substantially free of outside pressure and able to concentrate fully on what they are doing. Whatever the task may be, whether it is art, writing, music, sport, or science, it is almost within the range of their usual capabilities, so that they have the basic skills to perform it, but, at the same time, they are challenged to extend their limits. This means that close concentration is necessary, not in a way that brings them anxiety but because they find in such close application a sense of delight. So close is the identification of the doer and the deed that it is almost as though the activity performs itself. It flows. In such a state of consciousness distractions are easily banished so that the person is fully immersed in the action. And time flies.

Meanwhile, there is some process of internal feedback that communicates a sense that everything is going well. An experienced archer may know that the arrow is on course even before it reaches the target—because it feels right. When a person acts in a state of flow, the activity is usually of a high standard, objectively speaking. Subjectively it is the source of happiness, creativity, satisfaction, fulfillment. Often enough success does not lead to pride or arrogance, because the person feels that what was done was performed under the influence of something larger than themselves, before which they can feel only humility. Writers sometimes gratefully attribute their work to their muse's inspiring them as they wrote. The work itself, as well as its aftermath, is relatively free of egotistic demands. To some extent it is autonomous; it stands apart from the ordinary demands of everyday life.

18. New York: Harper and Row, 1990.

The state of flow is usually reserved to those with a certain clarity about the goals in their lives, and these shape their motivation so that what they do under their impulsion is self-motivating, or autotelic. This clarity enables them to exercise a high degree of self-control in the conduct of their day-to-day existence. The Olympic swimmer rises early to train; the concert pianist renounces many alternative pastimes to practice. Those who are committed to using their gifts keep expanding their universe in an ordered and systematic way, developing their skills and resisting the ever-present temptation to dissipate their energies on things that do not matter. They are practitioners of leisure, not of idleness. We may think of someone like Mozart as one who was naturally gifted, who did not have to do much to display his dazzling talents. Yet he himself would probably not agree with this, since we know he was critical of the following generation for dissipating their energies and wasting their time. Even prodigious talent requires nurturing and hard work. We are not always magnanimous enough to recognize this. The diva Joan Sutherland traveled everywhere with her voice coach, allowing no day to pass without considerable time spent in practice.

An appreciation of flow demands of us a recognition of the nobility of human labor. Notwithstanding the message that some receive from the Genesis account of the Fall, I am uncomfortable with the idea that work should be regarded as a penitential exercise. Nor am I a particularly ardent admirer of that kind of mindless work in which there is no need for workers to invest themselves, so that their minds are free to wander, even if such work permits them to graze in lofty spiritual meadows.[19] There is nothing inherently defective about honest human work that needs to be remedied by adding something to it. Most communities would prefer that the monastic cooks not burn the dinner; they are indifferent to

---

19. This seems to have been the case envisaged by the Cluny customary, where work was ritualized: processions, psalms, readings were superadded to such mundane tasks as working in the garden, as though the work itself had no inherent meaning except that which was added to it.

whether, in their midst of vegetable preparation, they were swept up into the ecstasy of mystical *excessus.*

The nobility of work was celebrated by Pope John Paul II's encyclical *Laborem exercens* of 14 September 1981. He speaks of the inherent dignity of work and of its need to be subordinated to human values: "Work is a fundamental dimension of human existence on earth." And "Work is a good thing for man—a good thing for his humanity—because through work man *not only transforms nature,* adapting it to his own needs, but he also achieves *fulfilment* as a human being and indeed, in a sense, becomes 'more a human being.' "[20]

> *The primary basis of the value of work is man himself,* who is its subject. This leads immediately to a very important conclusion of an ethical nature: however true it may be that man is destined for work and called to it, in the first place, work is "for man" and not man "for work." Through this conclusion one rightly comes to recognize the pre-eminence of the subjective meaning of work over the objective one. Given this way of understanding things, and presupposing that different sorts of work that people do can have greater or lesser objective value, let us try nevertheless to show that each sort is judged above all by *the measure of the dignity* of the subject of work, that is to say the person, *the individual who carries it out.*[21]

Quality work has a special significance in the life of celibates. As we are aware, there are three major sexual needs that emerge in a man's lifetime, probably overlapping one another to a certain extent: genitality, intimacy, generativity. In mid-life, especially, generativity is important. Men want not only to create something unique, but to leave behind something that bears the impress of their signature. This is vital to their sense of well-being, their con-

20. John Paul II, *Laborem exercens,* §9.
21. John Paul II, *Laborem exercens,* §6.

tentedness with monastic life, and their ability to endure the sorts of hardships and idiocies that all of us experience occasionally. It sometimes happens in monasteries—especially those dedicated more explicitly to the enclosed contemplative life—that there are relatively few possibilities for truly generative activities available. As a result, monks are allowed to exist with their talents underdeveloped and underemployed. This is not good for them, because it often leads to their wasting their lives on trivialities. And it is not good for the community, because underdeveloped talents can quickly fester into a generalized dissatisfaction with monastic life and a tendency to subvert or undermine initiatives that aim at clarifying and reinforcing the fundamental priorities of the group.

Why does it happen that the talents of monks and nuns are left undeveloped? Sometimes it is because the demand of income-generating occupations is total, and there is no time left for activities that do not contribute directly to the income stream. Sometimes opportunities are restricted to those favored to be within the superior's circle of approval: their needs and gifts are appreciated, and doors are opened for them. The needs of those outside this circle can be effectively ignored through pastoral indolence, through a kind of vindictiveness, in which they are punished for being less than totally ecstatic about the superior's performance, or through envy in which their giftedness is seen as a threat to the prevailing mediocrity.

Of course, whatever work is done, things sometimes go wrong—perhaps through a lapse on the part of the worker, perhaps through the unavoidable effects of external circumstances. Difficulties in work constitute a universal element of real life. If we are resilient enough to deal with the situation instead of seeking to blame others or to reproach ourselves, no great harm is done. Most of us have experienced that character is both built up and recognized when people have to deal creatively with negative situations, whether these are due to themselves or to others. To the extent that we are oppressed by our reverses we can do what all Christians do, we can take our difficulties to prayer and allow the healing balm of quiet time with God to ease our chagrin and to bring us to a calmer space—and perhaps, at the same time, to teach us a little lesson of detachment and purity of intention!

It happens in monasteries that sometimes we are assigned bad jobs—work for which we are unsuited or untrained, or work that everybody else has successfully avoided. In such situations, we have to find our security and satisfaction in other areas of our lives so that we are not unduly affronted by some sense that the work is unworthy of us. Perhaps we may not reach the level of equanimity that Saint Benedict envisages in his sixth and seventh steps of humility, but, if we can recover our peace and put our best into the work, we may well find that things are not as dire as we had anticipated. And, who knows, we may find contentment in the unwelcome tasks and even a little enjoyment. Joyless good works are, in the last analysis, of no real utility to anyone.

Each of the works that we do has its own rhythm that is not always accessible to observers. Most tasks lie somewhere on a spectrum between inspiration and perspiration; sometimes there is no holding us back, and, at others, we can scarcely move at all. As a writer, I am aware that words sometimes flow easily and at others that nothing comes and it is better to find something else to do. Asked from where he gets the material for his books, the American writer Don De Lillo remarked, "It comes out of all the time a writer wastes."[22] This implies that "wasting time" is an integral part of the creative process of writing. My own experience is that often taking a break or being interrupted is sufficient to start the words flowing again.

In our hyperactive world, it is probably useful to reconsider something of the monastic teaching on leisure.[23] Saint Benedict will

22. David Remnick, "Exile on Main Street: Don De Lillo's Undisclosed Underworld," *The New Yorker*, 15 September 1997, 43.

23. On this see Michael Casey, *Strangers to the City: Reflections on the Beliefs and Values of the Rule of Saint Benedict* (Brewster, MA: Paraclete Press, 2005), 26–37; *Grace on the Journey to God* (Brewster, MA: Paraclete Press, 2018), 147–59.

probably not forgive me for changing one word in his opening
sentence of the chapter about work: "Idleness is the ~~enemy~~ energy
of the soul"! To shoehorn the maximum amount of work into the
time available is not necessarily a virtue. More often than not taking
a break will improve both the quality of the work and the disposition
of the worker. Here there is no need for me to say more than that
there is a role for recuperation and relaxation in monastic life,
though, obviously, it should not become a fulltime occupation.

Sometime overwork is a more serious problem in monasteries
than idleness; this is especially so as manpower decreases and
monastic populations are aging. New entrants may not necessarily
provide a solution, as often they are given assignments to suit their
own particular needs, while the capacity to service the needs of
the community remains the same. A diminished workforce is not
the only source of a tendency to overwork. It sometimes happens,
either during a time of personal transition or over an extended
period, that a monk becomes disenchanted with the spiritual components of monastic *conversatio* and participates in them as little
as possible. Personal prayer and *lectio divina* are downsized first,
and then participation and punctuality at the Liturgy of the Hours
begin to suffer, and even the Eucharist begins to slip away. All
due to the demands of work; at least, this is what is claimed. One
may be forgiven for suspecting that work is expanding not according to its own necessities but to fill the gap left by a much-reduced
involvement in spiritual exercises. A similar phenomenon may be
noted when work is used as a means of avoiding participation in
community life, whether it concerns either formal gatherings or
informal encounters. Sometimes even meals are skipped. It can
happen, especially ten to twenty years after profession, that a
monk is bitten by the bug of ambition and so begins to work with
a view to bettering his standing either in the community or among
outsiders. Work becomes all-important and other areas of monastic
observance are left to stagnate. "The last temptation is the greatest
treason, to do the right deed for the wrong reason."

I think that when Saint Benedict speaks about the "labor of
obedience" (Prol. 2) he is using *oboedienti*a as a general reference

to the whole of the monastic *conversatio* rather than to the specific notion of doing what one is told. Its opposite is *desidia*, a word that is derived from *sedere*; it means sitting around and doing nothing. We need to remember that the primary work of the monk is his monastic life; the tasks he has to do, whatever they be, take their context and meaning from being part of his monastic living, no less essential to the integrity of *conversatio* than the other elements. May I recall the remark already quoted from Cardinal Braz de Aviz at the Abbots' Congress in 2012: Sometimes "we must have the courage to diminish our works to save our charism." Especially in these days when many communities are operating with reduced numbers, it is important that we avoid letting our workload increase to the point where the monks seem not to have either the time or the energy for the essential activities of the monastic day.

Maybe Qoheleth was right, and we should concentrate on finding enjoyment in our work, giving thanks that we have the opportunity to utilize and develop our talents as well as being of service to others. And we should be grateful that Saint Benedict has devised a system whereby there is the possibility for the blending and alternation of activities so that each of us—probably in our own way—can arrive at some kind of dynamic balance that provides the foundation for a lifetime of stability.

Perhaps we might give the final word to Saint Isidore of Seville (560–636) from the chapter on the work of monks in his *Regula monachorum*:

> The monk should never despise being involved in any work that is necessary for the monastery's way of life.
> The patriarchs pastured sheep. The gentile philosophers were stitchers and tailors (*sutores et satores*), and the righteous Joseph to whom the Virgin Mary was espoused was a

worker in iron. So also Peter, the Prince of the Apostles, was a fisherman, and all the apostles did bodily work so that they might support the life of the body.

So persons of such great authority gave themselves to tasks and labors, even rustic ones. How much more should monks, for whom it is right not only that they should produce the necessities for their own lives by their hands, but also by their labors provide relief for the indigence of others.

Those who are strong of body and in good health are known to sin in two ways if they are indolent; for not only do they not work themselves, but they prevent others from working and invite them to imitate their indolence. Therefore let any who enter monastic life (*quisque convertitur*) be careful to serve God by their labor and not to be filled with slackness and sloth by being given over to idleness.[24]

The possibility of working is a great blessing for monks and nuns. "Work is an occasion for a fruitful asceticism that fosters personal development and maturity. It promotes health of mind and body and contributes greatly to the unity of the whole community."[25]

---

24. Isidore of Seville, *Regula monachorum* 5:2–3; PL 83:873–74.
25. *Constitutions OCSO*, §C.26.

8

Self-Restraint

It sometimes surprises people to hear that one of the most important factors in building community is the willingness of each member of the community to restrict and, in some cases, renounce self-interest in favor of a common advantage. Another way of stating this principle is to point out that self-centeredness is toxic in any group, and narcissism makes cohesion impossible. Those who enter the micro-community of marriage soon learn that give-and-take is essential if the relationship is to blossom. The community does not exist for the singular benefit of one person, like the staff of a high official. The purpose of community is to create an ambience in which all the members jointly enjoy a better life. There is, however, a deeper consideration. As with every other aspect of Christian living, the grace of monastic community is stamped with the seal of the paschal mystery. There is the prospect of a more abundant life, but the entry to it is through experiences that sometimes seem like death.

The advantages of living in community are clear. Essential tasks can be shared among many, so that there is more leisure, more time to think of creative solutions, more time to complete tasks well. There is a possibility of pooling knowledge and experience, and there is scope for collaboration on tasks too great for one. The result is an incremental growth of knowledge from one generation to the next. Occasional geniuses can contribute to improve the lives of others. In more complex groups, the resultant development of culture allows for the emergence of "objective culture"—visible improvements in the standard of living through science, technology, engineering, and manufacturing. When this happens, it has the effect of increasing the quality of "subjective culture" in each person—the possibility of enjoying the "benefits of civilization" with the ideal outcome that people become more fully human and alive.

A functional group grounds the possibility of affective community and lays the foundation for the intimacy that supports and energizes each member in their participation in the life of the totality. Vague sentiments of togetherness are no substitute for the serious efforts required if persons of different temperaments and competencies are to live and work together on a long-term basis. No community can exist for long unless a strong majority of its members are prepared to exercise a good measure of self-restraint.

An individual may be born to a group, but continuance in the group is not automatic. Although some animal groups encourage individual existence to increase the prospect of survival of the species, normally the best prospect for individuals is to be part of a larger entity. To run with the herd means voluntary acceptance of group standards and, in particular, its structures of dominance. This necessarily involves curtailment of some individual possibilities. The individual will must yield to the common will.[1] The advantages of group membership are considered greater than the disadvantages in conforming to social rules.

Sometimes monastic communities are slow to admit that monastic life is challenging, despite Saint Benedict's instruction that prospective candidates be warned about the *dura et aspera*. Apart from the attraction of an easier life there is a fear that aspirants will be discouraged from entering if the monastic life is presented in all

---

1. During the Covid-19 pandemic we saw examples of persons who claimed to be "sovereign citizens" and refused to comply with restrictions enacted for the common good. Such people quickened the spread of infection, causing others to become ill and some to die.

its austerity. Perhaps the opposite is the case. Newcomers are often characterized by (sometimes excessive) fervor. They are not so interested in half-measures. The monastery is a "school of the Lord's service"; there is no room for those who don't want to learn or, to express it differently, who don't want to accept the restrictions and struggles that are a part of every learning process.

Sociological studies have revealed that strict demands "strengthen" a church. Laurence Iannaccone sees this happening in three ways: they raise commitment levels, they increase participation, and they enhance the net benefits of membership: "The strength of strict churches is neither a historical coincidence nor a statistical artefact. Strictness makes organizations stronger and more attractive because it reduces free riding. It screens out members who lack commitment and stimulates participation among those who remain."[2] This is not to suggest that the way to strengthen a monastery is simply to make the life more austere. A classic study of the 1960s has demonstrated that there must be a dynamic interplay between comfort and challenge. It is worth pondering whether, to some extent, the conclusions drawn are applicable to monasteries.

> In sum, for the church to opt for either comfort or challenge as its principal task seems unreasonable. One might suggest, then, that the church seek to redress the balance between the two functions. Since the church's performance of a comforting role now overshadows its efforts to challenge, why not try to put a little more backbone in the latter, while maintaining a commitment to the former. . . . Nonetheless, redressing the balance is no simple solution.[3]

---

2. Laurence R. Iannaccone, "Why Strict Churches Are Strong," *American Journal of Sociology* 99, no. 5 (March 1994): 1180–1211 at 1180.

3. Charles Y. Glock, Benjamin B. Ringer, and Earl R. Babbie, *To Comfort and to Challenge: A Dilemma of the Contemporary Church* (Berkeley: University of California Press, 1967), 209.

If we ask why people are prepared to embrace a hard life, the answer must be sought in a compensating experience that makes all the sacrifices involved not only tolerable but—mysteriously—desirable. Perhaps they instinctively understand Dietrich Bonhoeffer's assertion that there is no cheap grace. The acceptance of the gift of grace makes demands upon us. We can no longer continue the kind of life that satisfied us previously, which means leaving our nets and our family behind and following Jesus. That is only the beginning of the renunciation; it continues all through life.

When persons enter intentional communities, their attachment to the group is not due to an accident of birth or to an arbitrary assignment by others, but it is the result of a free choice on the part of the individual. This is made on the basis of embracing the group ideal and being willing to employ the means offered by the group to attain that goal. This often means accepting a new identity, part of which will be defined or refined by the group. Beyond participation in group activities, it involves the willingness to cultivate the appropriate beliefs and values that sustain group practice.

It is important to recognize that all who join a monastery give up something precious in order to be part of the community. To live a monastic life requires not only leaving family and friends and giving up personal possessions, but it also demands a different attitude to sexuality, a different attitude to authority, a different attitude to self-assertion, and a different attitude to others. Above all entering monastic life means affirming a belief in the spiritual world and a hope to attain eternal life. Without eschatological expectation, renunciation makes no sense. Living open to the mystery of the spiritual world involves assigning only relative importance to what is seen, touched, and heard.

To become a member of a community involves concrete renunciations that are dramatic at the beginning, but remain quietly demanding all through life. Chapter 58 of Saint Benedict's Rule insists that the candidate must renounce:

1. His dignity, enduring the difficulty and indignity of entry. (3)

2. The easy life: he is warned of hardship and roughness ahead. (8)

3. His security, since his continuance is subject to probation. (11)

4. His freedom of movement. (15)

5. His freedom: henceforth he will be subject to the Rule. (16)

6. His property and his potential inheritance. (24)

7. His power over the body. (25)

8. His hair (see RB 1.7) and his own clothes. (26)

9. And even his personal name. (See RB 63.11-12)

A snapshot taken on the day of entry is no longer valid after profession, twelve months later. Everything about the candidate's exterior has changed, and it is to be hoped that the process of interior transformation is also well underway.

Abba Paphnutius made the point that there are three levels of monastic renunciation.[4] It begins with leaving behind our family, our home, maybe our country, our career, and whatever wealth was ours in order to take up the monastic life. But at this point the renunciation is only beginning. Throughout our monastic career we need to deny our instinctual tendencies and change our customary daily behavior, and to struggle against our vices—both bodily and spiritual. The process of allowing grace to integrate our lives and to permit us to grow in purity of heart will continue until we reach the threshold of heaven. But meanwhile we are also being called to be drawn away from the world of sense into the spiritual sphere. A "passion for the unseen" (*invisibilia concupiscimus*) that leads to ecstatic prayer involves the standing aside from all merely sensible and rational reality in an act of supreme self-transcendence that culminates in the act of leaving

---

4. John Cassian, *Conferences* 3.6; SCh 42:145.

the world of space and time and entering into everlasting life. This is the ultimate stage of renunciation. We let go of life itself and allow ourselves to be drawn into eternity.

Renunciation continues throughout monastic life, although its degree of drama fades as good habit and delight in virtuous living render monastic *conversatio* easier and more natural (RB 7.68-69). There is a progression from conscious effort to the ease of habit and, thence, to a genuine delight in virtue. Saint Bernard terms this transition the passage from *disciplina* to *natura* to *gratia*.[5] The progressive facility in virtue that it manifests, however, is also an ongoing and increasing summons to give increasing priority to the interior life at the expense of alternative occupations and preoccupations that have no everlasting significance. The higher we rise, the more self-restraint is demanded. Spiritual growth is not an invitation to diminish our efforts. When we are called to rise above our station we are conscious of our need to be attentive. We may be able to relax by drinking with friends at the local pub, but if we are honored to be invited to a highly exclusive club, our enjoyment will be muted by our need to make sure we don't make too many *faux pas*. And when we are summoned to Buckingham Palace to take tea with the queen, concern to do the right thing will probably blot out any sense of pleasure we might otherwise have felt. So, in monastic life, when we are called to associate with the angels we have to watch our steps. The more spiritual we become the more self-restraint becomes part of our life. Because we are called not only to "seek the better gifts" (1 Cor 12:31), but also to seek those that are above (Col 3:1), this will involve a lifetime of effort and a generous receptivity of grace.

Sometimes it is easier to appreciate the value of a particular course of action by looking at its opposite. In the case of community living, we can see in a systematic lack of renunciation a

---

5. See Bernard of Clairvaux, SC 23.6; SBOp 1:141. On this text see Michael Casey, *Athirst for God: Spiritual Desire in Bernard of Clairvaux's Sermons on the Song of Songs,* CS 77 (Kalamazoo, MI: Cistercian Publications, 1988), 250–51.

cause of considerable malaise. It is signaled by narcissistic attitudes, tepidity, behavior inconsistent with monastic life, a chronic tendency to conflict, various forms of acedia including the overuse of and overreliance on social media, a generalized lack of commitment. The interplay of these symptoms often leads to situational depression and, eventually, alienation and departure. Living in a community in which such behavior is countenanced is difficult, because slackness tends to be contagious, as the history of monasticism amply illustrates. It is hard to be faithful to one's commitments when infidelity is all around; to do so means setting oneself apart from the community and exposing oneself to the dangers of arrogance, self-satisfaction, and singularity.

We are all familiar with a term that the ancient monks borrowed from Stoicism: *apatheia*. The word does not mean "apathy"; it is not indifference, but a powerful and positive attitude that could perhaps be best rendered "equanimity" or "even-mindedness," both understood as dynamic. *Apatheia* is a determined effort to remain unruffled by changes in external circumstances. If in some situations this is beyond possibility, then it is a question of returning to tranquility as quickly and as completely as possible. In Cassian's reprocessing of the term it came to be associated with "purity of heart," understood as a single-minded pursuit of the goal that left no scope for pursuing alternative objectives. In a cenobitic context, *apatheia* involves a deliberate refusal to be upset by any of the idiocies that common life delivers so generously, but to have a firm resolution to respond thoughtfully rather than to react automatically to what is happening around us.

As monks and nuns grow spiritually they tend to become less interested in the doings of others and the politics that often surround community decision-making. They attend to their work and mind their own business. The tentative burgeoning of interior prayer often means that they are more drawn to a quiet life and less inclined to participate in the kind of conversation that eventually and unwittingly undermines the solidarity of the community's members by distinguishing an in-group (us) from an out-group (them). Any reduction in the common obstacles that hinder a group's progress in the direction of unanimity is worthwhile, even though it is merely the by-product of a more fundamental fidelity. In this way, *apatheia* can be viewed as a source of community harmony, reducing assertiveness, reactiveness, and tendencies to rash judgment that are among the most usual inhibitors of the growth of a genuine community spirit.

If it is true, as Saint Aelred writes, that "the perfection of monks consists in setting aside self-will,"[6] then it is probably also true that the setting aside of self-will is among the most fundamental requirements of any who wish to build a pleasant and functional community. The condemnation of self-will—*voluntas propria* as distinct from *propria voluntas*[7]—is commonplace among monastic writers of all centuries. Saint Benedict returns to this theme several times in the course of his Rule.[8] Here are some early examples:

1. [Regarding Sarabaites] "Their law is the pleasure of their desires: whatever they think or choose, this they call holy: and what they do not want they consider unlawful. (RB 1.8)

2. [Regarding Gyrovagues] "Always wandering and never stable, serving their self-will and unlawful appetite for food." (RB 1.11)

3. "In all things, therefore, all are to follow the rule as master and nobody is to deviate from it rashly. None in the monastery is to follow the will of his own heart." (RB 3.7-8)

---

6. Aelred of Rievaulx, Sermon 43.5; CCCM 2A:337.

7. "Generally we can say that in patristic literature *propria voluntas* is seen more positively as 'one's free will' rather than only self-will and willfulness" (Aquinata Böckmann, *From the Tools of Good Works to the Heart of Humility: A Commentary on Chapters 4–7 of Benedict's Rule* [Collegeville, MN: Liturgical Press, 2017], 59). The conclusion is drawn from a study of the occurrences of *voluntas* in the works of Augustine, Ambrose, and John Cassian.

8. See Terrence Kardong, "Self-Will in Benedict's Rule," *Studia Monastica* 42, no. 2 (2000): 319–46.

4. "To hate self-will." (RB 4.60)

5. "And so they seize the narrow path, of which the Lord said, 'Narrow is the path that leads to life.' They desire to have an abbot over them so that not living by their own judgments nor obeying their desires and pleasures, they walk by the judgment and rule of another and live in communities." (RB 5.11-12)

6. "The second step in humility is if persons do not love their own will and do not delight in satisfying their desires." (RB 7.31)

Cenobitic life is lived under a rule and an abbot or abbess and can be understood as an overarching negation of self-will. The fact remains, however, that even with the advent of detailed customaries, not every single action was regulated—there was some scope for a response to individual needs and wishes. When the emphasis passed from enforcement to personal responsibility, the zone of choice was expanded, and, for some, monastic *conversatio* became almost completely unboundaried.

There are two themes in the writings of Thomas Merton that may help us to understand the role played by the renunciation of self-will in bonding persons together in a warm monastic ambience. The first is his distinction between the "deep" or "true" self and the "superficial" or "false" self. In this context, it is the false self that is restrained and renounced in order that the true self may be liberated. The second theme concerns his recycling of Saint Bernard's teaching on the "common will," according to which self-will is de-prioritized in favor of what is decided by the community.[9]

Let us begin by recapitulating some of his ideas about the true and false self with a view to understanding the distinction that he is making and the inference he draws regarding the authenticity of a life:

9. See Michael Casey, "Merton's Teaching on the 'Common Will' and What the Journals Tell Us," *The Merton Annual* 12 (1999): 62–84.

> Every one of us is shadowed by an illusory person: a false
> self. This is the [person] I want myself to be but who cannot
> exist, because God does not know anything about him. . . .
> My false and private self is the one who wants to exist out-
> side the reach of God's will and God's love—outside of real-
> ity and outside of life. And such a self cannot but be an
> illusion.[10]

The superficial sense of self is the result of social conditioning
whereby we receive our identity from others—our genes, our
name, our culture, our education, our training. To a large extent
we become what others make us, and we identify ourselves by
the way in which others regard us. If we fulfill their expectations,
we receive approval and affirmation; to the extent that we do not,
we are most often rejected and disavowed.

The false self is governed by the pursuit of pleasure and the
avoidance of pain; it has no ambition beyond maintaining and
enhancing its own status quo. There is no sense or desire for self-
transcendence. This inauthentic self is the engine that drives all
our sinful tendencies: "A life given to the cultivation of this
shadow is what is called a life of sin."[11]

> All sin starts from the assumption that my false self, the self
> that exists only in my egocentric desires, is the fundamental
> reality of life to which everything else in the universe is
> ordered. Thus I use up my life in the desire for pleasures
> and the thirst for experiences, for power, honor, knowledge,
> and love, to clothe this false self and construct its nothing-
> ness into something objectively real.[12]

In those cultures where shame is an important mechanism of
social control, it is very difficult to become aware of a sense of

10. Thomas Merton, *New Seeds of Contemplation* (London: Burns & Oates,
1962), 27.

11. Merton, *New Seeds,* 27.

12. Merton, *New Seeds*, 27–28.

self-identity beyond this group-induced identity. To depart from the course approved by precedent and followed by one's neighbors demands a large amount of courage and determination.

There is a major transitional point in our life when we begin to make our choices not on the basis of the approval of others but in accordance with conscience and the promptings of the interior Spirit. At this point we have begun to be aware of something that is glimpsed only infrequently at first, but that has the capacity to seize our attention and to begin to redirect our lives. Its power is not in some future promise but in the grounded reality of who we are:

> The inner self is not an *ideal* self, especially not an imaginary, perfect creature fabricated to measure up to our compulsive need for greatness, heroism and infallibility. On the contrary, the real "I" is just simply ourself and nothing more. Nothing more, nothing less. Our self as we are in the eyes of God, to use Christian terms. Our self in all our uniqueness, dignity, littleness and ineffable greatness. . . . [Our] real and "homely" self, and nothing more, without glory, without self-aggrandizement, without self-righteousness and without self-concern.[13]

This authentic self is the only basis of fully free human activity—otherwise we are just responding to the conditioning we have received. In the first place, it is the basis of any experiential relationship we have with God. Jesus criticized the Pharisees precisely for their playacting: religious observance had become a substitute for genuine human interaction with God or with neighbor. Remember the parable of the Pharisee and the tax-collector at prayer. One was truly himself; the other was offering a false image of who he was.

The blossoming of the deep self does not happen without the elimination of its more visible rival. For the true self to flourish,

---

13. Thomas Merton, "The Inner Experience: Notes on Contemplation (I)," *CSQ* 18, no. 1 (1983): 3–15, here 9.

the false self must be put to death. Self-actualization is subject to the demands of the paschal mystery:

> In order to become oneself, one must die. That is to say, in order to become one's true self, the false self must die. . . . [This involves] a deepening of the new life, a continuous rebirth, in which the exterior and superficial life of the ego-self is discarded like an old snakeskin and the mysterious, invisible self of the Spirit becomes more present and more active.[14]

> Unless we discover this deep self, which is hidden with Christ in God, we will never really know ourselves as persons. Nor will we know God. For it is by the doors of this deep self that we enter into the spiritual knowledge of God.[15]

The contemplative life, in whatever degree it is present, depends on the activation of the authentic self. Genuine community has also the same requirement. The ideal of monastic community can be realized only by persons who have attained a good level of authenticity. Otherwise community life becomes a pantomime of amateur actors, pretending to be something they are not, observing the niceties while underneath there is neither solidarity nor respect. Such communities exist.

It is in recognizing the integrity of others that we are sometimes led to forsake our own judgment and subdue our desires for the sake of harmony, and, if we have made any advance in humility, we may recognize that sometimes others know better than we do. To be a peacemaker in community will often involve bridling our self-will and, sometimes, as Saint Bernard adds, silencing our self-counsel, so that conflict is avoided. The good thing about such acts of virtue is that they are unseen by others and so not likely

14. Thomas Merton, *Love and Living* (New York: Farrar, Straus and Giroux, 1979), 196, 199.

15. Thomas Merton, *The New Man* (London: Burns & Oates, 1962), 30.

to be done for the purposes of enhancing our reputation or adding fuel to our ambition.

Like the double commandment of love, self-will takes two simultaneous forms: it is resistance to any intrusion that may be considered an expression of the will of God, and it is a chronic refusal to assign any importance to the preferences of the many. Self-will is the opposite both of obedience to superiors and to the mutual obedience that Saint Benedict recommends. This duality is well captured in Saint Bernard's description of self-will:

> Self-will is that which is not common either with God or with human beings but is solely our own; [it occurs] when what we will is not for the honor of God nor for the utility of the brothers [and sisters]. What we do is for our own sake with no intention of pleasing God or being of benefit to our brothers [and sisters] but to satisfy the particular movements of [our own] souls.[16]

The term "common will" seems to have been original to Saint Bernard.[17] The common will offers a means of verifying the integrity of one's choices and offers an antidote when these are somewhat toxic. Just as taking counsel is a means of checking the reliability of one's own perceptions, paying attention to the common will can help us to arrive at a deeper level of purity of intention. The malice of self-will consists not in the choices made but in the fact that these choices are made without reference to or in

---

16. Bernard of Clairvaux, Res 3.3; SBOp 5:105. The last clause is difficult to translate: *satisfacere propriis motibus animorum.*

17. Thus Edith Scholl, "A Will and Two Ways: *Voluntas Propria, Voluntas Communis,*" CSQ 30, no. 2 (1995): 191–204, at 196. In fact, the CETEDOC concordance indicates that this was not a common usage in Bernard's writing. See also Irénée Rigolet, "Contribution au 'vocabulaire' cistercien: Voluntas propria, Voluntas communis," *Collectanea Cisterciensia* 55 (1993): 353–63. And Thomas X. Davis, "Cistercian *Communio,*" CSQ 29, no. 3 (1994): 291–329; see especially the section on 314–17.

opposition to the will of God or to the will of the community to which one belongs.

Perceptively, Bernard sees "self-counsel" as conjoined to this willful independence from God. Self-counsel consists in having strong opinions that are not based on knowledge or reason. Such a misinformed state becomes dangerous because opinions are elevated into principles and used to crusade for particular courses of action, even though these are considered ill-advised by most. The internet is a wonderful source of fake knowledge and deluded advocacy. I know of a monk who was convinced that the use of aluminum cooking vessels was the cause of Alzheimer's disease and irritated everybody by constantly calling for their removal. I know of a nun who was convinced that eating animal products was itself sinful and was, in addition, the cause of even greater sinfulness; she annoyed many in her community by her ongoing vegan advocacy. There are other less obvious cases, where individuals believe themselves to be the only one in the community with access to the truth and so become progressively alienated from the rest.

> [*Proprium consilium*] is what belongs to those who have a zeal for God but not according to knowledge. They pursue their own error and are stubborn in it so that they do not want to agree with any advice that is given them. They cause division where there was unity, they are the enemies of peace, they lack charity, they are swollen with vanity, pleasing themselves and being great in their own eyes, ignorant of the righteousness of God and wanting to set up their own [in its place]. What greater pride is there when one person prefers his own judgment to that of the whole community as if he alone had the Spirit of God?[18]

Thomas Merton first wrote of the common will when he was asked to translate a document from the OCSO General Chapter

18. Bernard of Clairvaux, Res 3.4; SBOp 5:106–7.

of 1925 and add some pages of additional commentary.[19] As with many of his earlier writings, when his relationships with superiors (in this case Dom Frederic Dunne) was positive, Merton tends to be enthusiastically maximalist about obedience. His tendency toward collectivizing the common will seems to make of community policies a kind of *sensus fidelium* that is guaranteed to be God's will. This is further than Saint Benedict is prepared to go, since he recognizes that communities can go astray, even in important matters such as the election of a new abbot (RB 64.3-6).

Nevertheless, a moderate view of the idea of the dignity that is to be accorded to a will that is common to a majority of the community is a very useful adjunct as one continues the monastic journey. Perhaps another word that was much used by the early Cistercians could also be used to evoke this ideal: unanimity.[20] If we are to form a local expression of the church, we must aspire—at least—to being of one heart and one mind. To arrive at such a point demands of each a large measure of renunciation, expressed by self-restraint in acting and boundless patience in enduring. This is not a call to see our community merely as "the cross," as a trial to be borne. Certainly the common life is a challenge, but the root of the challenge is that it calls us to the integrity of Gospel living, and that will always be a source of deep contentment and personal fulfilment.

Patrick Hart has published a curious little booklet written by Thomas Merton for the young monks in his charge, on the topic

19. A Cistercian Monk of Our Lady of Gethsemani, *The Spirit of Simplicity Characteristic of the Cistercian Order: An Official Report Demanded and Approved by the General Chapter, Together with Texts from St. Bernard of Clairvaux on Interior Simplicity* (Trappist, KY: The Cistercian Library, 1948). Merton's contribution was republished in *Thomas Merton on St. Bernard,* CS 9 (Kalamazoo, MI: Cistercian Publications, 1980), 107–57.

20. See Michael Casey, "Unanimity First, Uniformity Second," in E. Rozanne Elder, ed., *Praise no less than Charity: Studies in Honor of M. Chrysogonus Waddell, Monk of Gethsemani Abbey,* CS 193 (Kalamazoo, MI: Cistercian Publications, 2002), 123–40.

of "Monastic Courtesy." It was probably written in the early 1950s, at a time when Gethsemani often had more than a hundred novices in its midst. At times, it is almost laughable in its attention to detail, but the author's purpose is serious:

> Our Christian and monastic courtesy are marked with the sign of the Cross, because usually the acts by which we give evidence of good manners are of a kind to cost us some trivial sacrifice, in order to place others before ourselves. The bad-mannered person is usually selfish, and his bad manners are often clear indications of his selfishness.[21]

Monastic community is grounded on the massive, life-changing renunciations that signal its distinctiveness from other lifestyles, but it is also dependent on innumerable small actions whereby persons follow not what is useful to themselves but to others (RB 72.7).

In his address to the members of the General Chapter of the Strict Observance Cistercians on September 23, 2017, Pope Francis asserted that the three essential components of their vocation were constant prayer, self-restraint, and unity in charity.[22] Of self-restraint the pope said,

> From the outset, the Cistercians of the Strict Observance were characterized by their great *self-restraint* in life, convinced that it was a valid support in order to concentrate on the essential and to more readily attain the joy of the spousal encounter with Christ. This element of spiritual and existential simplicity preserves its entire value of testimony in today's cultural context, which too often leads to the desire for ephemeral goods and illusory, artificial paradises.[23]

---

21. *The Merton Annual* 12 (1999): 13–21, at 15.

22. A different triad, deriving from Pope John Paul II, was enunciated by the abbot of Tilburg: Joy. Prayer. Community. See Bernardus Peeters, "Sfide e segni dei tempi," *Vita Nostra* 19 (2020): 14–26.

23. *Osservatore Romano* [English Weekly Edition], November 10, 2017, 10.

Of course, self-restraint is necessary if individuals are to live harmoniously in community, but there is also a corporate aspect to this value. We live in an acquisitive and competitive society where a lot of energy is expended on getting more of everything. To practice the simplicity about which the pope spoke we have to review our corporate attitudes to poverty and property. Most monasteries are rich by local standards, with vast landholdings, extensive buildings, and large capital reserves. To manage such precarious assets, counsel is sought from those who are wealthy and successful. This is prudent; most of us are relatively inexperienced in high finance, and we are under an obligation to safeguard what we have received from previous generations. At the same time, there is a hidden danger that unknowingly we may begin to absorb from these high-fliers attitudes that have more to do with rampant capitalism than with the Gospel. Administrators need to be consciously self-restrained in their approach to money, willing to be "poor with the poor Christ," limiting expenditure to what is necessary or useful and not falling into the trap of conspicuous consumption. This is especially important in those situations where income has lost contact with work and money flows in from investment portfolios. The fact that there is money available does not mean that it must be spent. A certain restraint is called for. As the *Exordium Cistercii* remarks, "association of possessions with virtue is usually not longlasting."[24]

Today we tend to speak less about penance and mortification because these terms have sometimes developed unhealthy and unnecessary mournful connotations. When we refer instead to self-restraint we envisage a voluntary and intelligent channeling of our personal or corporate energies with a view to an outcome that we accept as more important. It is not a negative term. It simply indicates that our heart and mind are in control of our lives

---

24. *Exordium Cistercii* 1.4; Chrysogonus Waddell, ed., *Narrative and Legislative Texts from Early Cîteaux* (Brecht: Cîteaux–Commentarii Cistercienses, 1999), 399.

so that the choices we make are not subverted by rampant sub-personal inclinations. Self-restraint is a good thing.

As with everything else, too much self-restraint is not a good thing. There is a time to be assertive and a time to hold back. In addition, we need to avoid becoming too lyrical about penance and mortification. Self-denial can sometimes be a subtle vehicle for self-hatred and even lead to a kind of masochism. Self-chosen penances ensure that what we do remains within the limits of our tolerance—we are always in control. The underground urges that really need to be monitored and checked remain untrammeled.

A much better arena for mortification is, as Saint Bernard notes, more passive: "Indeed, penance must be done, but this seems to be more a matter of what we endure than of action."[25] Tolerating the inevitable inconveniences and irritations of the common life without reacting negatively is a far less egotistical way of bringing self-will to heel.

In any case, the natural effects of aging, if accepted gracefully, can put a dampener on some of the worst effects of self-will and instinctual behavior. And a drift toward apophasis diminishes our desire to engage in discussion with a view to imposing our opinions on others. A sense that all is vanity, as Qoheleth insists, leads us away from the kind of issues that devour others and nurtures in us a willingness to leave everything in God's hands. Confidently leaving everything to God is the ultimate in self-restraint.

25. *Agenda utique paenitentia sed ad passionem hoc quam ad actionem videbitur pertinere.* Div 15.4; SBOp 6a:140. See also Div 2.7; SBOp 6a:84: *Non modo faciendi tempus est, sed etiam patiendi.*

9

Self-Truth

Humility is not the easiest topic to discuss because it is not always easy to separate the basic concept from the confusing connotations it has garnered over the centuries. In particular, when humility is regarded as an aspect of social interaction, it quickly becomes obvious that the gestures commonly associated with the action are often subject to multiple interpretations. Once, in a bus terminal in Seoul, I watched as a man approached a ticket-vending machine. He bowed to the machine, did his business, took the ticket, bowed again, and walked away. The bow was so meaningless that it had become invisible to him. It was a mere simulacrum of the attitude it was originally meant to embody.[1]

It must also be obvious that the various actions by which it is believed that politeness, courtesy, respect, deference, and friendliness are expressed are void of meaning if the corresponding interior attitude is lacking. To speak about humility and its role in lubricating community relations, some effort needs to be expended in coming to an understanding of the ample interior foundations of this value. When we speak about humility as something worth cultivating usually we are referring less to objective humility (lowly social status) or particular actions that bespeak humility,

---

1. To use the terminology of Jean Baudrillard.

and more about an inner attitude, termed by the New Testament *tapeinophrosune* (humblemindedness).

Many years ago I wrote a book on Saint Benedict's chapter on humility.[2] Instead of repeating what I wrote there, let me offer some alternative considerations on this important quality and on the way it tends to manifest itself and develop in the lives of those who follow the monastic way.

One

The study of the classical usage of the word leaves us in no doubt that humility (usually considered as status) was not highly prized in ancient cultures. We notice a difference in the Old Testament and, more sharply, in the New Testament. Humility comes to acquire a higher value because it is associated with an encounter with the spiritual world. To have stepped over the threshold of the spiritual world, even momentarily, is to have a new vision of reality and, correspondingly, a revised insight into our position within that totality. Friedrich Schleiermacher defined our standing in the face of absolute reality in terms of dependence.[3] We become convinced that our whole existence is dependent on that which is wholly other from the world of our experience. Even the merest trace of solipsism is delusional.

This apprehension of our unique relatedness in a larger universe inspires contrary emotions. On the one hand, we are filled with a desire to penetrate more deeply into the heart of the mystery we

2. Michael Casey, *Truthful Living: Saint Benedict's Teaching on Humility* (Petersham, MA: Saint Bede's Publications, 1999). In slightly improved form this was later reissued as *A Guide to Living in the Truth: Saint Benedict's Teaching on Humility* (Liguori, MO: Triumph, 2001).

3. Friedrich Schleiermacher, *On Religion: Speeches to its Cultured Despisers*, trans. John Oman (New York: Harper and Row, 1958), 26–101: "The Nature of Religion."

have glimpsed. On the other, we draw back, conscious of our unworthiness and of our earthly origin.[4] After all, according to the Book of Genesis, we were created out of dirt (*humus*); we are already ontologically humble. The recognition of this is a moment of self-truth that is the basis of genuine humility. The process of acknowledging our lowliness is complemented by an intimation of our inherent nobility. Astonished, humankind discovers itself to be a *nobilis creatura*. We discover our loftier potential as we own our attraction to spirituality and as we experience delight in it. It is because we are assured of our high calling that we are prepared to admit what in us is lowly. As Saint Bernard says, "It is from this first encounter of the reason with the Word that humility is born."[5] Spiritual experience has as one of its validating indicators a sense of one's littleness in the grand scheme of things. This interior attitude must itself be further guaranteed by the manner in which we begin to relate to ambient reality. We cannot continue as if nothing has happened.

The reserve we feel in the presence of God is different from ordinary fear because it is permeated by attraction and love. While recognizing the distance between us and the infinite, we also feel drawn to approach. Like Moses and the burning bush, we remove our shoes in reverence, but we go forward and seek to come closer

---

4. "The truly 'mysterious' object is beyond our apprehension and comprehension, not only because our knowledge has certain irremovable limits, but because in it we come upon something inherently 'wholly other,' whose kind and character are incommensurable with our own, and before which we therefore recoil in a wonder that strikes us chill and numb. . . . The qualitative *content* of the numinous experience, to which 'the mysterious' stands as form, is in one of its aspects the element of daunting 'awefulness' and 'majesty' . . . but it is clear that it has at the same time another aspect, in which it shows itself as something uniquely attractive and *fascinating*" (Rudolf Otto, *The Idea of the Holy*, trans. John W. Harvey, 2nd ed. [New York: Oxford University Press, repr. 1980], 28 and 31).

5. *Ex qua prima coniunctione Verbi et rationis humilitas nascitur* (Hum 21; SBOp 3:32).

to the mystery. The very strength of the attraction generates in us a certain tentativeness, as if we are afraid our brashness will spoil everything. If you were to give me an exquisite piece of Murano glassware, I would be delighted. At the same time, I would be terrified lest through inadvertence in handling it I drop it on the ground and it breaks. Delight and terror coexist. The greater the delight, the greater the terror.

It is in recognition of this eye-opening revelation of a transcendent universe that Saint Benedict identifies the first milestone on the journey to authentic holiness as "fear of the Lord." The comprehensive meaning of this biblical term is often underestimated. The feeling that has been generated by the discovery of a reality infinitely greater than the known world is closer to awe than to dread. Hilary of Poitiers (d. 368) clarified the matter in these words:

> Fear is not to be understood according to its usual meaning in human opinion. For such fear is the trepidation experienced by human weakness, afraid that it will suffer something it does not wish to happen. We feel this fear when confronted by a guilty conscience, by the law imposed by the powerful, by the attack of someone stronger, by an incident of sickness, by meeting a wild beast, or by suffering anything bad. Such fear is not taught us, but it is the outcome of natural weakness. We do not have to learn what we are to fear; the things we fear infect us with their own terror. . . .
>
> The fear of God must be learned; it is taught. Its teaching is not by terror but by reason, not from natural fearfulness but acquired from the keeping of precepts and from the works of an innocent life and through the knowledge of truth. . . . For us the fear of God consists entirely in love, and fear finds its completion in perfect love (*metum eius dilectio perfecta consummat*).[6]

There is always a certain ambivalence about the response we feel when drawn into the sphere of God. We are moving into a

6. Hilary of Poitiers, *Tractatus in CXXVII Psalmum* 1–2; PL 9:704.

zone where the normal rules of conduct are no longer sufficient. Instinctual reactions need to be subjected to scrutiny. We must pay attention; to relax is dangerous. This is why Saint Benedict describes this first step in terms of mindfulness:

> The first step of humility is always to place the fear of God before one's eyes and to flee from all forms of forgetfulness (*oblivionem omnino fugiat*) and always to be mindful of everything that God has decreed and always to turn over in one's mind how those who despise God fall into hell for sins and the eternal life prepared for those who fear God. (RB 7.10-11)

What is significant in this short quotation is that the word *semper* (always) occurs three times. In the continuation of this step *semper* occurs five more times (RB 7.13, 14, 18, 23, 27), *omni hora* (at every hour) four times (RB 7.12, 13, 13, 29), and *quotidie* (every day) once (RB 7.28). This seems to indicate that in Saint Benedict's mind not much progress in holiness is to be expected until this attitude of seriousness has become a permanent feature of one's approach to life. The dilettante will remain in the doldrums until something dramatic happens to break the deadly spell of inertia.

This insistence on laying solid foundations imparts a high level of sobriety to Saint Benedict's spiritual doctrine. Although such a change in direction usually indicates an intense experience of conversion, there is not much scope for enthusiasm. Instead, Benedict seems determined not to allow potential candidates to rush into a hasty commitment but instead to proceed step by step, weighing up the consequences of any decisions that are taken.

The same plodding beginnings are necessary in the learning of almost any art or trade. To arrive at self-truth, we must experience and cast away from ourselves many delusions, and resist the primal terror occasioned by standing naked and allowing others to see us as we are. There is a tendency in us to want to cover ourselves so that we are seen as we present ourselves and not as we are. We are like politicians whose public image must

be crafted in order to win general approval. And similar subter-
fuges are not unknown in religious communities, where the desire
to be called holy before we actually are is not unknown (see RB
4.62). Privacy serves a good purpose when it serves to avoid
publication of what is truly intimate, but when it is used to con-
ceal reality or to project a distorted or incomplete image, its
pursuit becomes an agency of bad faith. The norm to which we
aspire is that enunciated by Saint Paul: "Let no one think of me
beyond what is seen and heard from me" (2 Cor 12:6, cited by
Saint Bernard eleven times). What you see is what you get.
"Human beings," however, "see only what is on the surface, but
God looks into the heart" (1 Sam 16:7).

The fear of God is entirely distinct from the kind of fear by
which many are unknowingly beset. This hidden fear expresses
itself in an iron determination to maintain control: over oneself,
over one's reputation, over areas of responsibility, and, progressively, over what others do and what they are. Such compulsive
controllers may seem to have a strong personality, imposing their
will or their whim on all and sundry, but in fact they are weak,
fearful of what damage the unexpected may inflict. A truly strong
person is trustful of Providence and does not fear surprises. When
people seek to control they are also seeking to inhibit God's action
in the world; they are probably more influenced by a rampant
superego than by any experience of the transcendent. Their im-
patience is often coupled with an unrealistic perfectionism, in
which everything associated with failure or imperfection generates
in them a strong sense of discontent and restlessness.

Two

The journey to integral self-knowledge involves our gradually
finding our place in relation to God, to others, and to the world,
as well as reflexively establishing a credible self-assessment. Having a right estimate of where we stand in the world—or in the
community—is the necessary foundation for appropriate behavior.

Clearly our contact with ultimate reality sustains this process, as does our interaction with other people. We don't gain much self-knowledge merely by looking in the mirror.

The first result of having encountered the sacred is a reserve in following automatically all the inclinations that come from deep inside us. This frees us to discern which of the options before us is most life-giving. We recognize that there is more to reality than meets the eye. Those on the spiritual path quickly learn to give practical priority to what God wills over their personal desires, not because of some theoretical notion of scoring merit, but simply because doing so feeds the inward sense of God's presence. Each consciously chosen act that implements the divine will reverberates within, its intensity measured not by the objective quality of the action but much more by the subjective dispositions in which it was performed. Choices inspired by a single motivation necessarily have a stronger impact than those dispersed through multiple intentions. To offer a stranger a glass of water without ulterior motivation is superior to preaching a papal retreat, which, although it is done under obedience, brings with it a certain dubious notoriety that is liable to lead the saintliest souls into deeper delusion and thus pollute the crystal candor of the good deed.

Perhaps it is worthwhile to place a certain emphasis on the fact that the best way to upgrade our interaction with God is to have a zeal to conform ourselves with what is manifestly God's will. This doesn't mean that what God wills is always patently obvious. Sometimes we will have to search for it; sometimes we will have to grapple with conflicting claims. The determination to find God's will has the same effect as doing God's will; it re-orients our whole being toward God. And, inevitably, away from the selfish inclinations that are the source of so much unhappiness.

Three

In our pursuit to find a practical expression of God's will there are several strong contenders. The first is our conscience, especially when it is fired by the clear teaching of Jesus. It is not the text of the Bible alone that has compelling force; otherwise we would all have to pluck out our eyes and cut off our hands and feet. The word of God can be mediated by many different agencies, but it becomes efficacious in deciding a course of conduct only when it is welcomed in a faith-filled conscience. Otherwise, for all its inherent truthfulness, it remains outside, banging on the door and demanding admittance. Sometimes it may summon strong-arm friends to break in and force compliance, but the resultant behavior is not really a free response to God's self-revelation, but coerced and probably resentful.

There are many claimants to possessing and exercising exclusive rights over the interpretation of the word of God, notably the church's magisterium. Ecclesiastical authorities can forbid and even prevent the publication of teaching contrary to church doctrine, but they are unable to command a person to act against their conscience, even if that conscience is in error.[7] In the case of religious who have vowed themselves to the practice of obedience, that obedience is never absolute and unqualified. There are canonical and constitutional limits to what may be commanded, and, as long as these are respected, "a religious should not easily conclude that there is a contradiction between the judgment of his [or her] conscience and that of his [or her] superior."[8] Compliance

---

7. See the *Catechism of the Catholic Church*: "A human being must always obey the certain judgment of his [or her] conscience. If he [or she] were deliberately to act against it he [or she] would condemn himself [or herself]. Yet it can happen that moral conscience remains in ignorance and makes erroneous judgments about acts to be performed or already committed" (§1790). "If . . . the ignorance is invincible or the moral subject is not responsible for his [or her] erroneous judgment, the evil committed by the person cannot be imputed to him [or her]" (§1793). The distinction here is between ontic evil and moral evil. Jephthah's commitment to his vow obliged him to sacrifice his daughter even though it was painful for him and against God's law (Judg 11:30-40). Objectively what he did was a heinous sin, but morally he was convinced that he could do no other.

8. Paul VI, *Evangelica testificatio* §28.

with a command, however, need not be virtuous; it may simply be submission to a *force majeure*. When the consequences of disobedience are more painful than doing what has been ordered, not much merit results.

Obedience to superiors is best understood in the context of universal obedience—what Saint Benedict terms "mutual obedience." This is the faith-filled belief that everyone whom we encounter can be the mouthpiece of God, as Balaam's donkey was, pointing us in the direction of more abundant life. The emphasis is not on the jurisdiction of the one commanding or on the intrinsic value of the deed done but on the willingness to open one's heart and one's life to a potentially divine alternative.[9] Often the suggested course will cause us to change our plans, and none of us likes doing this. It is the willingness, after due discernment, to cede control over the direction of our life that is important. To journey through the years with such a disposition obviously has a transformative impact on the quality of one's interactions—with God and with neighbor.

In a monastic community, special deference is due to the superior's orders, on the supposition that these are oriented solely toward the good of the community or that of the individual concerned. Those fortunate enough to live in a community where there is widespread confidence that this is what actually occurs will be more likely to attribute only relative importance to their own perceptions and opinions and more readily accept the possibility that automatically following the dictates of self-will is not always a good idea. During a pandemic, it is no more than common sense to let go of one's preconceptions and preferences and to follow the advice of specialists. They may not always be right, but it is more prudent to pay attention to them than to follow unhesitatingly the promptings of our own untutored prejudices.

9. I have previously termed this attitude "antecedent willingness." See *Strangers to the City: Reflections on the Beliefs and Values of the Rule of Saint Benedict* (Brewster, MA: Paraclete Press, 2005), 91–105.

The monastery is an intentional community; people join it because they wish to advance toward the goal it proposes for itself. Those who lead it are meant to be skilled in furthering this progress. In Saint Benedict's way of looking at things, the abbot is meant to be a professional in searching out God's will, applying it to each particular situation, and communicating it in a manner that is likely to be persuasive. Where such confidence reigns there will be a high level of peace in the community and a general acceptance that life is heading in the right direction.[10]

When considering the spiritual advantages of monastic obedience, it is important not to limit one's attention to the superior as a manager, who makes practical dispositions about things to be done or omitted. A monastic superior is primarily a leader, pointing the way to reach the goal for which members of the community joined. This is why Saint Benedict gives priority to teaching and the making of policy over merely giving orders. Obedience in a monastery is not what is expected in the army. It is an openness to be led beyond the parameters of self-assessment to a more abundant life. Of course, this places a huge onus on superiors. Alas, many of them are incapable of filling such a role and tend to limit themselves to managerial functions, putting up notices and keeping everyone moderately happy. Perhaps it is helpful to remember the kind of ideal relationship sketched out in the anecdotes from the Desert tradition. Disciples sought and received a word of wisdom to guide their progress; the *abba* or *amma* was concerned solely for the welfare of the one who had approached them; nothing else mattered. Of course, governing a community is a bit more complicated. A monastic superior needs skill, not only in determining the most life-giving option, but also in the willingness to embody it in their own manner of living. Beyond

10. But care is always needed. Warren Buffet once said, "It takes twenty years to build a reputation and five minutes to ruin it." Quoted in Stephen M. R. Covey with Rebecca R. Merrill, *The Speed of Trust: The One Thing That Changes Everything* (New York: Free Press, 2006), 131.

this, the relationship with members of the community will habitually fall short of the ideal unless the superior has a high degree of empathy. When hard things are enjoined or a permission refused, the superior needs to feel interiorly something of the pain and frustration of the other person.

A superior according to the mind of Saint Benedict is one who, more by deeds than by words, encourages the members of the community to have confidence in the effectiveness of taking to heart what others—and especially the superior—have to contribute. Gruff, unapproachable abbots may pride themselves in running a tight ship, but their monks will usually look elsewhere for spiritual guidance and inspiration. Inevitably this will make the monks more beholden to what Saint Bernard terms self-counsel, inasmuch as they choose the advice they will follow by their choice of adviser.

One who catches a glimpse of God begins a journey to find God, less as an external object to be sought than as an energy to be absorbed. In a sense, the person is not searching for God but seeking to become like God, to be transformed by the divinizing light into a new creature. It is an ontological journey and pursuit. This trajectory begins by making serious efforts to give oneself to be formed more completely by God's self-revelation, whether this is a matter of entering more deeply into one's own inner experience or allowing oneself to be shaped by providential forces external to oneself that are expressive of the divine Word. The process is of less concern than the end result.

Four

This malleability under the hand of God may bring to mind the prophet Jeremiah when he visited the potter's workshop (Jer 18:1-10). There often seems to be a succession of cycles in one's monastic life in which one is made and then broken, and then remade and then rebroken. Having once yielded control, all semblance of predictability seems to fade from one's life, and it becomes imperative to base all one's security on the fidelity of God, not on one's own capabilities or the good will of others. Candidates to monastic life are warned that the way to God is sprinkled with *dura et aspera* (RB 58.8), and veterans are in no doubt that this is true. There are several levels in which patience will be tested. Difficulties are due to more than human malice. Embracing the common life means accepting to live with those who are profoundly different and whose behavior may be perceived as puzzling, at best, and offensive at worst. Living under a rule demands that we detach ourselves from many personal preferences and conform to common norms. Having a superior means that there is no guarantee that the situation in which I have comfortably settled today will continue indefinitely. Regarding the details of my exterior circumstances I have no unassailable certainty. To the extent that I derive my identity from the work I do or the position I hold, it will seem that I am to live forever on the brink of impending doom. As one of our venerable seniors was wont to mutter, "Abbots have tremendous power."

The answer is, of course, that I have to develop an interior security that allows me to weather any storms that come my way. This means having a firm trust in a divine providence that can write straight on crooked lines. If we have sincerely refused to place an absolute value on our own ideas about the future direction of our life, we are less likely to be upset when these optimistic projections go awry. Persons whose security is anchored in God do not suffer less because of their external misfortunes, but their outward suffering causes less mental conturbation, because faith in God gives context and meaning to what they are enduring. Like Saint Paul they may be led to affirm, "I calculate that the sufferings of this present time are not worthy to be compared with the glory that will be revealed to us" (Rom 8:18). And: "These slight, momentary afflictions of ours are bringing about a surpassing and enduring measure of glory" (2 Cor 4:17). And, from the Epistle to the Colossians: "Now I rejoice in suffering on your behalf, and

I bring to completion in my own flesh what still remains for the afflictions of Christ on behalf of his body, the church" (Col 1:24). This is not some caricature of Stoicism; it is a firm belief that everything is in God's hands and that "for those who love God all things work together unto good" (Rom 8:28).

Hard times activate faith, hope, and charity. Any battle-scarred monastic veteran will tell you that. What doesn't kill you will make you stronger. Our experience of the spiritual world assures us that there is more to life than what happens in the here and now. This inspires in us a hope, not so much that things will get better, but that ultimately all will be well. And having experienced the love that created us and surrounds us, we find joy in returning that love in contrary circumstances.

Joy is the key. In the Epistle to the Colossians, the author speaks of the empowerment Christians receive: endurance (*hupomone*), patience (*makrothumia*), and . . . joy (Col 1:11). There is a sequence here. Hard times come upon everyone; if we are to survive we have no alternative but to endure them, but even that requires a measure of fortitude. Then, if we are able to see our suffering in a spiritual context, we will be able to remain calm during the storm, trusting in the providence of God to bring things to a creative solution. If our faith has truly penetrated our whole person, then, like the apostles, we will rejoice to have been found worthy to suffer for the name of Jesus (Acts 5:41). Even if we do not attain that height of indifference to pain, in retrospect we will likely feel like sounding the trumpet to proclaim, "In all these things we overcame because of God who has loved us" (Rom 8:37).

What hard and contrary things are likely to be encountered in the course of a monastic lifetime? Mostly these are the common sufferings of humanity: limitation, weakness, accidents, opposition, rejection, sickness, senescence, death. When Saint Benedict speaks of "undeserved injuries," he seems to be referring to something more malicious. The monks at Vicovaro tried to poison him. He himself explicitly forbids assault (RB 70). The records of the Cistercian general chapters through the centuries testify to instances of insult, assault, grievous bodily harm, attempted murder, and murder.[11] It would have been pleasant to report that such incidents are unknown in contemporary monasticism.

Saint Benedict speaks of false brethren, persecution, and being the object of cursing. Do monks and nuns ever experience persecution within their communities? Before we answer with a resounding negative, perhaps we should take into account that these may take a form somewhat subtler than what Saint John of the Cross experienced. In all my travels, I have never encountered a monk or nun who has been unjustly flogged and incarcerated. I have met people, however, who considered themselves to have been the targets of prejudice and discrimination. This can take the form of sidelining those who are unfavored, denying them opportunities to be generative, refusing to allow them to exercise their talents for the benefit of the community and to develop as persons, sometimes by burdening them with occupations that no one else wants. And I have heard accounts of controlling persons slowly sliding into bossiness and thence to what can only be described as bullying.[12] There are monasteries where it seems to be imprudent to give public expression to alternatives to prevailing policies. Of course, I realize that sometimes I am hearing only one side of the story and that in many cases there may be reasonable explanations for what has happened, but this reservation does not totally allay my concern for those involved. And I know that persecution is not always from the top down; it also proceeds in the opposite direction.

It is in such cases that long-term patience kicks in.[13] Patience implies an ability to see beyond present painful circumstances

11. See Michael Casey, "The Three Pillars: Filiation, Visitation, General Chapter," *Analecta Cisterciensia* 70 (2020): 398–99.

12. See Gerald A. Arbuckle, *Dealing with Bullies: A Gospel Response to the Social Disease of Adult Bullying* (Strathfield, NSW: St Paul's, 2003).

13. See Michael Casey, "The Virtue of Patience in the Western Monastic Tradition," CSQ 21, no. 1 (1986): 3–23; reprinted in *The Undivided Heart: The Western Monastic Approach to Contemplation* (Petersham, MA: St Bede's Publications, 1994), 95–120.

and to view them in the context of a positive outcome. Sick people become *patients* when they begin receiving treatment, because what is done to them, no matter how invasive it may be, is done in view of a better future. In such circumstance the virtue of patience means concentrating on the hopefully beneficial outcome more than on the suffering of the present moment. And it involves a large measure of trust in those conducting the treatment.

In a similar way, when hard times happen, when we have done all that is reasonably demanded to mitigate the severity of the situation, we need to learn to look beyond present unpleasantness in the confidence that, however great the malice of the secondary agents of our misfortune, we remain in the hands of God, who will not allow us to be tried beyond our limits. There are several tributaries that flow into this broad stream of confidence. At a basic level, we can usually say to ourselves, "This also will pass." More loftily, we can accept our pain as part of humanity's lot: I am human, and therefore suffering will not be absent from my life. Such an attitude imposes a restraint on our zest for pleasure and, ideally, generates in us a greater degree of empathy with the sufferings of others, however different from ours these may be. We may see ourselves as participating in the passion of Christ, as Saint Benedict indicates (RB Prol. 50). Inspired by the Beatitudes, we may be fired up with eschatological zeal, secure in the hope of a divine reward. Maybe it helps to be just a little bit stubborn, gritting one's teeth and muttering, "This thing is not going to get the better of me." It is gratifying to emerge victorious from our troubles, but, in the last analysis, it is sufficient simply to survive. What keeps us from total collapse is that encounter with the spiritual world that brought us to enter the monastic life—it seems so long ago. The total truth about myself is much broader and longer-lasting than what I endure at this hour.

Genuine patience is not an invitation to become a doormat. Nor are we obliged to condone objective unfairness or injustice. It is unreasonable to expect one who assigns a high priority to personal integrity to be unfeeling when that integrity is wrongfully impugned. Even if nothing is manifest on the outside, we may appreciate the sentiment expressed in Dylan Thomas's poem: "Do not go gentle into that good night . . . . Rage, rage against the dying of the light." Under a placid exterior a holy rage may burn for a time until its energy is transformed into something more creative. Eventually it may demand to come forth in prophetic denunciation, calling lies "lies," and abominations "abominations,"[14] but for the time being all is quiet on the western front.[15]

Five

Patience demands a good level of self-identity, and, moreover, it increases and strengthens that sense. Life in community is considerably easier when the members of the community are real people and not merely actors playing some pious role. Standing naked before the community takes a lot of courage. From our first days after entry we were encouraged to put our better foot forward and to project our most presentable face to the community. The result is that others tend to relate to our aspirational self rather than to our real self. And each positive response beamed toward that as-yet unrealized self makes us more discontented with the unseen reality. "If only they knew." For a long time, perhaps, I am very careful that no one catches sight of me when I am not wearing my public image.

Sometimes this role-playing expands. To hide a single truth about myself I have to block any reference to matters that might give a clue about what is being concealed. If I want to avoid public knowledge of my criminal record, I have to be purposefully vague

14. To paraphrase Karl Barth speaking of Martin Luther.

15. This kind of righteous wrath is to be distinguished from infantile tantrums, which, more often than not, are an expression of disgust at the disparity of power and an attempt to reconfigure the relationship. See Mary Margaret McCabe, "Thinking with Anger: The Value of Emotion in our Critical Thinking," *Times Literary Supplement* 5991, 26 January 2018, 11.

about the years before my entry into the monastery. If anyone asks an innocent question they will be surprised by the vehemence with which I withhold an answer. Meanwhile my body language and a growing tendency to obfuscation in speech will soon alert anyone observant enough that there is something being concealed. They are not meeting the real person, but only a stand-in. The relationship inevitably becomes strained.

Playing a part is tiresome, and eventually the mask begins to slip, and this causes alarm all around. In fact, the seeming disaster is good news, because it brings out into the open some of the uncreative inclinations that are an ongoing part of my character. Their publication means that I don't have to pluck up courage to talk about them; they are already widely known. If I can find someone in whose counsel I have confidence, the opportunity to talk about the hitherto hidden zones of my life is a great blessing.

Sharing my secrets with a trusted soul-friend marks a significant step forward in the spiritual journey. Disclosure is never complete, but with each covering cast aside I become more sure of my identity, affirmed as it is by the caring acceptance of another. When my most shameful failings are included in the package and these do not provoke rejection, a deep peace results. But the comfort of knowing who I am brings a challenge. I need to learn to act from this identity, to find the freedom to move aside the expectations of others and give priority to my own enlightened conscience. To be true to myself.

In the first place this means recognizing my own giftedness. Many people who think of humility in terms of self-denial are usually surprised to hear that this is an important aspect of that quality. To own my talents is part of self-truth: to believe that whatever I have is what I have received is its counterpart. A gift is gratuitous; it is given without predisposing worthiness. To own my giftedness brings with it a triple obligation: to develop my talent, to use my talent, preferably for the benefit of others beyond myself, and not to claim credit for what I have not earned. If what I have is a gift, then my attitude to it must be seasoned with a good measure of gratitude. Unless, in rare cases, it is done for a higher purpose, to deny or diminish my giftedness is to sin against nature.

When I recognize the precious strands of my natural giftedness I experience a deep sense of security that enables me to withstand the blindness, weakness, and malice of others. It is a source of strength that is of inestimable value. It means that I am less inclined to assert myself, since I don't have to prove anything. And if there are still pockets of delusion that might cause me to deviate from complete truthfulness, my openness with a soul-friend will help to identify these and negate their influence.

When I become less competitive I am more likely to appreciate the giftedness of others. I am quick to praise—not as a form of patronage, but as a genuine gesture of solidarity. It is high virtue to be grateful for the gifts of others, and it is an effective means of neutralizing the malign tendency of envy that nests inside us all. What a grace it is when I realize that the gifts of one are given to all; when another member of the community excels in something, the quality of life in the community is enhanced, and I share in that benefit. On the other hand, it may be noted that sometimes a community that contains many gifted members can be seriously divided. It is as though the different gifts were mutually exclusive. Unacknowledged giftedness almost always becomes toxic, whether it be through rancid competitiveness or in the subtle tactics of polite passive aggression.

A good level of self-knowledge is a social asset. Not only does it encourage me to serve others through my particular gifts, but it teaches me to sidestep situations in which my negative energies will be activated. It is especially helpful if the one from whom I seek counsel is a member of the community, whether it be a superior, a spiritual senior, or somebody else. This means that any situation I describe may already be known to them, and they can help me to arrive at a balanced interpretation of events. Too often, when monks consult outside directors or supervisors, the only side of the story that is told is their own, in which case it is easy to present themselves only as innocent victims, when everyday observers would be aware of a certain level of complicity.

While it is recommended that we let ourselves be seen as we are by other members of the community, this does not mean that the whole community should—metaphorically speaking—be walking around naked. There is no need for everyone to know the whole story behind everybody else. There is scope for privacy.[16] The non-concealment that Saint Benedict recommends ought to be practiced only with regard to those who know how to heal their own wounds as well as those of others. More often than we might expect, behind the pretty face a tragedy lurks. Not everyone is emotionally equipped to deal with full disclosure. While it may improve our relationship with the person, knowing their trials and traumas is, more often than not, a burden. They say that "a trouble shared is a trouble halved," but this means that those who have a fair degree of empathy are almost overcome by the sufferings of others. It means living with a strong sense of one's impotence to do much more than listen attentively and not to reject. Perhaps the only solution to be found is embracing the other person's hardship with the arms of our prayer.

Six

People comfortable and at home within themselves don't need a lot of accessories to render their lives tolerable. The necessities of life are adequate. Saint Benedict seems to suggest that if these are guaranteed then there should be no cause for anyone in the monastery to fret about not having enough. He also notes that there is a tendency to regard the possession of abundant and high-quality goods as a symbol of higher status.

The key word that Saint Benedict uses is *contentus* (RB 7.49); to be content with what one has subverts every desire to have more. When in 1770 Captain Cook and his men gifted the Guugu

16. As Dorothy Day remarked, "Privacy was part of the works of mercy," in Kate Hennessy, *Dorothy Day: The World will be Saved by Beauty: An Intimate Portrait of My Grandmother* (New York: Scribner, 2017), 285.

Yimithirr people of North Queensland with a selection of western clothes, they were later astonished to find them abandoned, "left all in a heap together, doubtless as lumber not worth carriage."[17] Who needs clothing in the tropics? Saint Jerome's dictum *nudus nudum Christum sequi* was not intended to be taken literally, but it does suggest that the accumulation of material goods, or rather, the desire to accumulate, is a serious impediment to heartfelt discipleship and even to an ordinary level of human happiness.

Naomi Klein has stated incisively, "We don't shop for what we buy; we shop to fill a hole."[18] So we end up with much more than we need, even with much more than we can use. The recognition of the futility of hoarding has been at the heart of Marie Kondo's campaign to rid our homes of whatever does not bring us joy. The same priority seems to animate the more somber Swedish ideal of *Döstädning* (death-cleaning), whereby we rid ourselves of whatever others will have to throw away after our deaths. The more we have, the more inherent potential for disorder. If I have five books, I can usually find the one I want; if I have five thousand, the task becomes more daunting. The more material things on which I rely for happiness, the greater the likelihood that there will be conflicting claims on my affection. The external multiplicity of possessions leads to inner dividedness. The only way for me to achieve simplicity of purpose is to reduce my attachment to the array of goods that presently clamor for permanent residence in my heart. If I am content with a few things, then I will be unencumbered by them. I will be free. And it will not be so difficult for me to be content.

A person who is content with little will blend easily into the life of the community. Conversely, the person with a strong sense

17. Thus Joseph Banks in his journal. Quoted by Peter Fitzsimons, *James Cook: The Story of the Man who Mapped the World* (Sydney: Hachette, 2019), 360.

18. Interviewed by Philip Adams in Radio National's *Late Night Live* on October 28, 2019.

of entitlement will always be making demands, always aggrieved that those demands are not met as expansively as possible, always envious of those who seem to be more amply rewarded. High-maintenance monks and nuns have a strong impulsion to feel special; usually they have lost the capacity to distinguish between needs and wants, and, as a result, their happiness is in jeopardy as soon as anyone does not totally defer to their urgent whims.

High standards regarding food are another manifestation of this lack of sensible detachment. When other sources of gratification diminish, monks and nuns sometimes compensate by taking more interest in the quality of their food, or they become self-styled connoisseurs of wine. By their superior standards of taste they demonstrate that they are a cut above the rest of the community. Incidentally, there is no evidence that it was because the wine offered him by the monks of Vicovaro was an inferior vintage that Saint Benedict rejected it.

Those who have committed themselves to the spiritual pursuit quickly realize that it involves a certain reserve with regard to the means of social communication. And while it is almost impossible to interact with the rest of humanity without access to such media, there is no real necessity to have the latest electronic gadgets and the status they confer. Saint Benedict's principle about clothes can be applied here: "Of these things let the monks not make an issue regarding their color or grossness, but let [them be] content with what can be found in the region in which they live or can be bought more cheaply" (RB 55.7).

Parallel to this love affair with material goods and the status they imply is a desire for an employment that brings enviable perquisites and a measure of public esteem. The problem is that in most monastic communities there are only a few jobs that meet these requirements. It is not unknown that those who have set their hearts on rising to these heights are often disgruntled at being assigned lesser occupations. Dissatisfaction or disempowerment in work situations is a major cause of discontent, depression, and even rebellion, especially among men. In most cases of ambition it seems that those afflicted by this consuming passion have lost sight of the goal for which they entered the monastery and for which they abandoned their (undoubtedly) brilliant careers.

Although ultimately it is the sense of acceptance by God that liberates us from the need to keep adding to our visible resources, freedom from the tyranny of acquisition is often a function of early family life. When children are loved unreservedly and unconditionally they grow up more relaxed; their self-esteem remains relatively distinct from status-conferring additions. Children who are reared in households where they have to compete for affection are more likely to yearn for visible tokens of worth to bestow on them the security they do not feel. As in other areas of monastic life, the degree of struggle experienced is often a reflection of these early formative years in the family.

Seven

Low self-esteem is not virtue. Indeed, as a form of false humility (*tapeinophrosune*) it was twice rejected as dangerous by the author of the Epistle to the Colossians (Col 2:18, 23).[19] Authentic humility is not some form of self-hatred powered by a deep, underground negativity; it is a realistic recognition that in many areas others are more competent than I am.

Sincerely to think of oneself as lower and less valuable than others need not be self-denigrating. When I played the cello alongside Pablo Casals, I readily affirmed that I did not play as well as he. When I climbed Mount Everest with Sir Edmund Hillary, I had no trouble admitting that his mountaineering skills were superior to mine. Although I won two gold medals at the last Olympics, I am happy to confirm that there were many who won more. Admitting the truth does me no dishonor.

19. The term is used in its usual positive sense in Col 3:12.

Such an attitude demands a certain generosity of spirit that enables me to recognize the good qualities in others, especially when it concerns qualities that I do not have or possess only to a lesser degree. In some cases, it may involve my vacating an assumed superiority in recognition of another's greater expertise. It is honesty. It is truth. When a brother wins a Nobel Prize, it is churlish of me to pretend indifference. Affirmation is the lifeblood of a flourishing community. The ability to recognize and celebrate our neighbor's giftedness is a most desirable social quality in situations where, too often, familiarity breeds contempt, and prophets are not welcomed in their own countries. Acceptance and admiration lead to gratitude, and communities are blessed when their members are quick to offer expressions of admiration and sincere thanks for services rendered.

The late Lord Jonathan Sacks, formerly the Chief Rabbi of Great Britain, speaks about the greater part of humility being "the capacity to admire . . . to be open to something greater than oneself. False humility is the pretence that one is small. True humility is the consciousness of standing in the presence of greatness."[20] How much happier we would be if we learned to admire those around us, instead of constantly emphasizing their defects. Admittedly, the practice of admiration is not easy when the everyday flaws of others are in such prolific abundance. This does not excuse the tendency by which we are absurdly ready to add to any compliment made of others the adversative conjunction *but*: "He may play the organ well, but he desperately needs a haircut." Magnanimity requires that we not allow inevitable imperfections disproportionately to obscure the radiant virtues or skills of those around us. It sounds easy, but it is not. Through some perversity that most of us experience, there seems to be an innate preference for perceiving the faults of others and for not allowing ourselves to be warmed by their good qualities. We are

20. ABC Religion & Ethics program of June 14, 2018. Downloaded from abc. net.au on July 5, 2019. See also *The Tablet*, 1 April 2000, 451.

unconsciously comparing ourselves with others much of the time. There seems to be an itch in us constantly to prove—mainly to ourselves—that we rank higher than those around us.

At the basis of this negativity there is a tendency to perfectionism. We ourselves are its first victims. Those who are plagued by this ambition are constantly goaded by a submerged quasi-parental voice urging them not only to try harder but also to do better, to achieve visible results. This inability to accept the reality of imperfection is a sore trial to the whole community. In Japanese culture there is an expression *wabi-sabi* that extols the beauty of what is imperfect, humble, and modest. In such a context striving for "perfection" may be taken as blasphemous, a Promethean attempt to scale heights humans were never meant to climb. Sometimes perfectionism is linked with some degree of obsessive compulsive disorder, sometimes it is the result of being brainwashed by a hyper-moralistic spirituality that relies more on guilt than on the grace of God. But it is a tendency that needs to be identified and laid low. Perfectionism is a sin against the common life; we desire to appropriate and reserve to ourselves the perfection that rightfully can only belong to the community.

No doubt perfectionism is connected with a Pelagian and semi-Pelagian attitude that Pope Francis identifies with a will lacking in humility:

> Those who yield to the Pelagian or semi-Pelagian mindset, even though they speak warmly of God's grace, "ultimately trust only in their own powers and feel superior to others because they observe certain rules or remain intransigently faithful to a particular Catholic style." . . . Ultimately, the lack of a heartfelt and prayerful acknowledgement of our limitations prevents grace from working effectively within us. No room is left for bringing about that potential good that is part of a sincere and genuine journey of growth.[21]

---

21. Pope Francis, *Gaudete et exultate* §49–50. See also *Evangelii gaudium* §94.

A deliberate policy of giving of priority to others is not the outcome of some psychological defect, but flows from fidelity to basic Gospel teaching. It is the foundation of a spirit of mutual service that has the capacity to bring much joy to a community. It is what Jonathan Sacks termed "the silence of the ego," which allows us to find our true place in the community to which we have come not to be served, but to serve:

> Man now subordinates himself to others in service. This has nothing to do with self-disparagement or servility. In such *tapeinophrosune* others are taken seriously because God himself takes men seriously and refers them to one another by His acts. Only by *tapeinophrosune*, refraining from self-assertion, can the unity of the congregation be established and sustained. Without *tapeinophrosune* it would crumble.[22]

Eight

The common rules and expectations of most monastic communities today leave room for a certain amount of initiative and individual flair. Only in the most tyrannical of communities is daily life heavily scripted. Most communities prefer a lighter touch, even though high expectations may remain. A normal expression of humility is the willingness to live within the boundaries that define the character of the community's lifestyle. These are not always carved in stone or codified; more often than not they are unspoken: invisible frontiers that appear only when we stumble across them. Growing into a particular community usually involves a capacity to intuit what is acceptable, and a tolerant acceptance of these often-arbitrary criteria.

---

22. Walter Grundmann, art. *tapeinos ktl,* in Gerhard Kittel and Gerhard Friedrich, eds., *Theological Dictionary of the New Testament* (Grand Rapids: Eerdmans, 1972), VII:22.

Failure in this respect does not matter much objectively. Who cares if a monk wants to wear his scapular back-to-front? Or eat his peas with a spoon? However, any deliberate gesture is significant subjectively. Resistance to custom is an act of passive aggression against the common way of doing things, often springing from a claim of exceptionalism ("The normal rules do not apply to me"), or from an underlying sense of grievance and resentment ("Nobody loves me anyhow").

It is interesting to note the seriousness with which Saint Bernard regards singularity in his treatise *On the Steps of Humility and Pride*.[23] This even though he depicts the monk beset by this vice as something of a joke. People consumed by their own need to be different often fail to notice how ridiculous they are becoming. We will have more to say about singularity in the following chapter.

The important value that singularity undermines is solidarity, a sense of truly belonging to the community and not merely living there, but consenting to be one of the common herd. More positively, solidarity teaches us to feel at home within the community. This means more than "This is where I live." Solidarity allows me to be defined by my membership in the community. When I speak of the community it is of "us" and not of "them."

Self-truth weans us from the cruel sense of exceptionalism that while placing us on a pedestal cuts us off from everything that is given us through our interaction with other people. Accepting our ordinariness is a giant leap, at which many of us balk even though, statistically, all of us must be close to being average. Hugh Mackay, the closest Australia has to a public intellectual, writes about the importance of solidarity:

> Most of us manage to be both honest and dishonest, to
> display both integrity and hypocrisy, and to confuse our
> own opinions with "the truth" in ways that make us look

23. Bernard of Clairvaux, Hum 42; SBOp 3:48–49.

ridiculous to people who happen to interpret the world differently. Humility helps us to understand all that. A dollop of humility could save us from much of the tension, bitterness and resentment that corrodes us, yet humility is desperately unfashionable at present; self-esteem is all the rage. . . . Perhaps in the process of accepting that we are the sort of people we truly are—messy, inconsistent, neurotic, as well as noble, earnest and endearing—we can find a new, more realistic level of respect for ourselves and each other.[24]

The opposite of solidarity is loneliness. Loneliness is not a function of being alone; many say they feel loneliest in a crowd. Loneliness has been described as an "emotion cluster," comprising elements of anger, resentment, shame, self-pity, sadness, and jealousy.[25] These are precisely the feelings that isolate people and cut them off from the support and affirmation that would otherwise be available to them. If such people would only detach themselves from their delusions of distinctiveness and join the crowd, not only would they find themselves happier, but it is probable that their spiritual lives and their efforts at prayer would run more smoothly.

Nine

People who lack humility often talk too much. An inability to silence the ego inevitably leads to talkativeness. Disguised as the communication of information or the celebration of friendship, talk can also be used as a means of dominating others, reducing them to silence through the unremitting repetition of the same

24. Hugh Mackay, "A Time for the Great Gift of Humility," *The Age*, December 21, 2002.

25. Fay Bound Alberti, *A Biography of Loneliness: The History of an Obsession* (Oxford: Oxford University Press, 2019).

monotonous monologues, in which the narrator usually plays a starring role. The body language of one who is trapped in such a situation often reveals their discomfort at being talked at for too long. Whatever information was meant to be conveyed has dissolved in a miasma of boredom, and, far from strengthening the relationship, this conversation has submitted it to duress.

The value of restraint of speech is recognized in many different traditions whether they be spiritual or philosophical.[26] Mahatma Gandhi, for example, was appreciative of the fact that his own natural shyness meant that he was often inclined to hold his tongue:

> I have naturally formed the habit of restraining my thoughts. A thoughtless word hardly ever escaped my tongue or pen. Experience has taught me that silence is part of the spiritual discipline of a votary of truth. We find so many people impatient to talk. All this talking can hardly be said to be of any benefit to the world. It is so much waste of time.[27]

"Silence is additional to, not a rejection of sociality."[28] Humble people are often good listeners; they respect others and hope to

---

26. There has been a spate of books on the topic of silence. Bilal Qureshi, "In a Noisy World, Books about Silence are Booming," *Washington Post Online,* March 12, 2020. Among them, Max Picard, *The World of Silence* (Wichita: Eighth Day Books, 2002); Sara Maitland, *A Book of Silence* (London: Granta Publications, 2008); Diarmaid MacCulloch, *Silence: A Christian History* (London: Penguin Books, 2013); Maggie Ross, *Silence: A User's Guide*, 2 vols. (London: Cascade, 2014, 2017); Erling Kagge, *Silence in the Age of Noise* (London: Penguin Books, 2018); Alain Corbin, *A History of Silence: From the Renaissance to the Present Day* (Oxford: Polity Press, 2018). This last was reviewed fairly negatively by Rowan Williams in *Times Literary Supplement* 6050, 15 March 2019, 44–45.

27. This passage is widely quoted but not referenced. I found it in Susan Cain, *Quiet: The Power of Introverts in a World that Can't Stop Talking* (London: Viking, 2012), 200.

28. Maitland, *A Book of Silence,* 13.

learn something from them. Their mode of being actively involved in fruitful conversation may be to say nothing. In other cases, they recognize—perhaps instinctively—that conversation has become a means of reinforcing existing power structures, in which case it is not truly bilateral, but an exercise in domination. The humble refuse to play such games: *nolo contendere*. As a result, their participation is less than enthusiastic. In both cases, not-speaking functions within the context of the relationship; it is not apart from it.[29]

There is another reason that people can move away from frequent conversation. We have already spoken about the monastic vocation as a consequence of an encounter with the spiritual world that has left a strong formative impression on a person's outlook on life. The strength of this impact waxes and wanes during a lifetime. When someone progresses in the spiritual life, the link with the spiritual world becomes clearer and more eloquent. It generates a need for a degree of withdrawal to ponder its implications or simply to submit to its charm. Talk about trivialities becomes less significant and is avoided if there is an option. This is done unselfconsciously and without any trace of criticism of others who are not now so much drawn to interiority.

It is probably true that those who feel impelled constantly to attempt to influence others do so because they harbor at least a smidgeon of doubt about the validity of their own opinions. When they are able to occupy the mental space of others and to convince them to change their minds, this feels good because their own uncertainty is (temporarily) assuaged. Those with a deepened linkage to spiritual reality don't need to convince others of anything. To them it is self-evident. If I look up into the night sky and see a full moon, I see what I see. There is no uncertainty. I don't have to hector others into the same conclusion. Look up and see.

---

29. [For students of language] "silence is a rhetorical device which is as much loaded with meaning as words are—if perhaps more in need of interpretation" (Stuart Sim, *Manifesto for Silence: Confronting the Politics and Culture of Noise* [Edinburgh: Edinburgh University Press, 2007], 10).

It is obvious. No argument can strengthen or weaken my perception. I see what I see.

In this approach refraining from speech is understood as being otherwise engaged. Silence thus appears as more than simply self-protecting from sinful discourse. It hardly needs to be remarked that to have attained such a state is usually a sign that solid progress has been made in silencing the ego so that the inward clamor to be heard begins to fade, and attention can be directed elsewhere.

It may be asked whether insisting on the connection between humility and silence does not unfairly burden extroverts, forcing them to act differently from their natural style. In a way it does, just as the discipline of cenobitic living invites introverts to come out from their shells. It is not just a matter of the suppression of natural inclinations, but of learning how to garner spiritual fruit from acting in a way that does not come naturally and has to be learned. In any case, the skills requisite for creative monastic living surpass the natural endowments of both introverts and extroverts. That is why Saint Benedict refers to the monastery as "a school of the Lord's service"—a school in which we are all learners, though the lessons we are taught vary. And he makes it clear to candidates that if they are not able to accept the discipline of monastic living they should seek their fortunes elsewhere.

The art of discerning the appropriate balance between speech and silence is something that all of us have to acquire, each in our own way. As Saint Gregory the Great reminds us, the challenges are different for different people:

> The taciturn are to be admonished in one way, those given
> to much talking in another. It should be suggested to the
> taciturn that while shunning some vices inadvertently, they
> are unconsciously involved in worse, for they often bridle
> their tongue beyond moderation, and as a result suffer in
> the heart a more grievous loquacity; and so, their thoughts
> seethe the more in the mind, in proportion as they restrain
> themselves by a violent and indiscreet silence. . . . But

those addicted to much talking are to be admonished to observe vigilantly from how great a degree of rectitude they lapse, when they fall to using a multitude of words . . . . Commonly since the slothful mind is brought gradually to a downfall by our neglect to guard against idle words, we come to utter harmful ones: at first we are satisfied to talk about the affairs of others, then the tongue gnaws with detraction the lives of whom we speak, and finally we break out into open slander. Hence provocations are sown, quarrels arise, the torches of hatred are lit, peace of heart is extinguished.[30]

When Saint Benedict recommends silence, the advice is directed to those wishing to pursue a spiritual life and whose endeavor has removed them somewhat from the busyness of the world to pursue a quieter life in a monastery. For such people, it is important that they be proactive in creating an interior silence that will, in turn, contribute to the quiet ambience that monastic living deserves.

Ten

Wisdom literature is usually sober, but it is also good-humored. Jean Leclercq once remarked to me that in reading Saint Bernard we should remember that his words were habitually garnished with a smile. Even when he seems to be sternly rejecting some aberration, he understood the importance of an ongoing *captatio benevolentiae*—the effort to maintain the good will of his readers and listeners. Mad rants alienate everyone. They may evoke fear, but they do not invite acceptance. Nobody would want to live in

---

30. Gregory the Great, *Regula pastoralis* III.14: *Quomodo admonendi taciturni et verbosi*; PL 77:71–73. Translated by Henry Davis, SJ, Ancient Christian Writers 11 (Westminster: Newman Press, 1950), 129–33.

a bleak and cheerless monastery.[31] Even worse is the feigned hilarity of deeply unhappy souls. As Caryll Houselander once wrote, "The forced smile of the amateur Christian is a blasphemy."[32]

There is a potential danger in trying to banish laughter from the monastery. Saint Thomas Aquinas asked the question whether there is a sin in a lack of playfulness:

> I answer that it must be said that in human affairs that which is against reason is vicious. Now it is against reason for someone to be burdensome to others, by offering no delight to others, and by hindering their delight. . . . Now those who are without playfulness are not only lacking in amusing speech, but are also annoying to others, since they are unmoved by the moderate mirth of others. Consequently, they are vicious, and are said to be harsh and boorish, as the Philosopher states.[33]

He continues by remarking that austerity, in so far as it is a virtue, does not exclude all delight, but only those delights that are superfluous and disordered.[34] He is, of course, influenced by the ancient philosophical appreciation of the virtue of *eutrapelia*.[35] Having previously noted that pleasure is delighting in that which is good,[36] he adds that those who devote much energy to

31. Thus, David Bell's efforts to puncture La Trappe's doleful image. For example, "Armand-Jean de Rancé: A Conference on Spiritual Joy," CSQ 37, no. 1 (2002): 33–46.

32. Caryll Houselander, *The Risen Christ* (New York: Sheed & Ward, 1958), 60.

33. Saint Thomas Aquinas, *Summa Theologiae* II-II, q. 168, art. 4c.

34. ST II-II, q. 168, art. 4, ad. 3.

35. Hugo Rahner, *Man at Play: or Did you ever practise Eutrapelia?* (London: Burns & Oates, 1965); Josef Pieper, *In Tune with the World: A Theory of Festivity* (Chicago: Franciscan Herald Press, 1965). *Eutrapelia* is mentioned only once in the New Testament, and in a negative sense: Eph 5:4. The Vulgate translated it by *scurrilitas*—the low-grade humor one would expect in vulgar domestic servants.

36. ST I-II, q. 25, art. 2.

intellectual or spiritual pursuits have need of periods of pleasurable relaxation:

> The remedy for weariness of soul must needs consist in the employment of some delight, by easing the tension of reason's study. . . . Now such words or deeds wherein nothing further is sought beyond the soul's delight are called playful or humorous. Hence it is necessary at times to make use of them to give rest, as it were, to the soul.[37]

Laughter is a quintessential human activity. To seek to banish laughter to an *aeterna clausura* (RB 6.8 = RM 9.51) is to create an inhuman community, from which human integrity will likewise be banished. This means that, if we wish to continue thinking of the Benedictine community as characterized by *humanitas*, it is necessary to add some qualification to the kind of laughter that is being excoriated. Certainly, excluding the *scurrilitates* mentioned in RB 6.8 would be no loss to anyone. Perhaps Saint Benedict is thinking more about the subjective attitude of the monk than about the act of laughter itself, because he cautions him not to be too easy and prompt to laugh. Laughter is not always a sign of spontaneous mirth and good humor; sometimes it is used as window dressing to disguise how the person really feels. I have seen people from certain cultures laugh when they make a stupid mistake in an effort to prevent their real feelings of exasperation or shame manifesting themselves. In discussion, laughter can be used as an unconscious means of distraction, to avoid going deeper into an area that the person does not wish to be explored. Because laughter is usually both spontaneous and contagious, the hope is that when the other person joins in the merriment, he or she will not pursue the clue that has been accidentally dropped. Certainly, not all

---

37. ST II-II, q. 168, art. 2. Following Cicero, he adds three qualifications: First, that the pleasure is not indecent or hurtful; second, that it does not upset the *gravitas* of the mind; third, that it is suitable to its situation.

laughter is to be rejected, but there are some forms of laughter that should attract a certain reserve or even suspicion. I may conclude this reflection with what I wrote twenty years ago: "There is probably no harm in postponing a campaign to eliminate laughter until some of our more significant vices have been curtailed."[38]

Eleven

A person with a good level of self-knowledge and a sure sense of identity usually leads a placid life, though not necessarily one immune from the standard trials and tribulations of human existence. This means that such people are less likely to feel the need to assert themselves and to dominate others. Their opinions are held lightly, and no need is felt to convince others of their correctness. This is why their withdrawal from debate is sometimes viewed as taciturnity. They do not need to be constantly reaffirmed. They do not need the spotlight on them. They feel no compulsion to gain the attention of others by clownish behavior. There is a certain steadiness to be observed in their interactions with others, a calmness that others may find exasperating. When they speak they do so briefly, seriously, reasonably. They are worth listening to.

This is the *gravitas* that Saint Benedict expected of a mature monk and that Paul VI, on a visit to Monte Cassino, praised so highly.[39] It is ponderous only when it is fake.[40] Authentic *gravitas* has a light touch. It leaves room for others; it does not subject their every word to visible and critical examination, and it feels no need to react when opinions contrary to their own are expressed. It is hospitable to who others are and to what they think.

38. Casey, *Truthful Living*, 230.

39. Discourse "Quale saluto," translated in *The Pope Speaks* 10 (1965): 120–26.

40. Like the *ophthalmodoulia hos anthropareskoi* (eye-service as people-pleasers) rejected in Col 3:22 and Eph 6:6.

Out of respect for others, those who are possessed by this quality of *gravitas* are somewhat reserved in pushing themselves forward. This may sometimes be a function of their unwillingness or incapacity to participate in conversations totally dedicated to the superfluous and flippant. It is not a decision made of the moment, but an enduring policy of self-insulating from the triviality that has invaded news outlets, the internet, and other social media. To have nothing to say in a conversation about the habits of venal celebrities is simply to refuse to become complicit in what has been termed "the globalization of superficiality."[41]

The stability vowed by the Benedictine monk is not only a commitment to remain a member of the community. It is not only a commitment to continue faithful to the common way of life. It is also an undertaking to grow in the stabilization of personality and spirituality that will ensure that visible perseverance is matched by the corresponding interior attitude. As this goal is being realized, the person imperceptibly loses interest in things that don't much matter and becomes somewhat more fixed on the *unum necessarium,* so that choices are made more by reference to the ultimate goal than under the influence of passing pressures. As a result, many issues begin to lose their strident urgency.

Twelve

Saint Benedict envisages the monk approaching the end of his journey as one in whom bodily and spiritual energies are in harmony. His response to grace is not dependent on where he is, or on his occupation. Monastic life has become so ingrained that even the observances he first found difficult become sweet, and

41. This is what Fr. Adolfo Nicolás, former general of the Jesuits, described as the most pressing problem of our time. In an interview with the then Australian prime minister, Kevin Rudd, quoted in *Late Night Live,* 6 November 2012. See abc.net.au.

faithfulness to the common life is now second nature. What he says with his lips he feels in his heart. There is no need for assertiveness or showiness; the ordinary, obscure, and laborious lifestyle of the common monk is glamorous enough for him. He is content.

What is happening is that prayer has, over the decades, slowly colonized his whole life. What began as an intrusive thought and flourished for an instant became more frequent, and then the instants coalesced to form islands of prayer in the prevailing sea of secular concerns. And very slowly great continents formed and prayer became, more or less fully, the monk's default state, to which he returned when nothing else was demanding his attention. This prayer brought him to an ever-deeper state of self-truth, in which his delusions were purged and a robust desire for God began to flex its muscles. He remains conscious of his long-lasting inconsistencies and his dithering about conversion, and he is unashamed to seek mercy and forgiveness. But his asking is confident because he knows that in making his petition he has already received that for which he is asking.

It has been quite a journey, but finally the monk has almost arrived at the goal for which he entered the monastery—and on this side of eternity!

10
Fellowship

In the *Politics*, Aristotle famously described human beings as societal animals. This means that association and sociable behavior are essential human activities, even in a monastery:

> The human being is by nature a societal animal (*politikon zoion*); an individual who is unsocial naturally and not accidentally is either of no importance or more than human. . . . Society is a creation of nature, which precedes the individual. . . . Anyone who either cannot lead the common life or is so self-sufficient as not to need to, and therefore does not share in it, is either a beast or a god. All are endowed by nature with the impulse toward community (*koinonia*).[1]

The Stoic philosopher Epicetus spoke of our social commitments in terms of fraternity, which we may equate with the gender-neutral "fellowship." By being willing to waive our rights in favor of others, we not only offer them a benefit, but we confer a benefit on ourselves, since in so acting we grow in virtue:

1. *Aristotelis Politica*, 1253a (Oxford: Clarendon Press, 1957), 3–4.

> After this, know that you are a brother also, and to this char-
> acter it is due to make concessions, to be easily persuaded,
> to speak good of your brother, never to make a claim in
> opposition to him in any of the things that are independent
> of the will, but readily to give them up. This is done in order
> that you may have the larger share in what is dependent on
> the will. Thus, for example, to gain for yourself goodness
> of disposition instead of a lettuce or a seat. This is no small
> advantage.[2]

I read in this text four characteristics of fraternity or fellowship that are to be sought in our interaction with those with whom we live.

a. To make concessions: to render services more readily and with less fuss than we would exhibit in dealing with strangers.

b. To be easily persuaded: to be convinced that a request made or an opinion advanced comes from an honorable person who has no cause to think ill of us and no reason to mislead us.

c. To speak well: since familiarity easily leads to contempt, it is easy to attribute exaggerated importance to minor quirks of behavior and allow these to dominate our conversation. A good means of peace-making is the determined effort to speak only good of those around us.

d. Not to be competitive: to give way and not to struggle to acquire more, or to have a higher reputation than our neighbors, and certainly not to make an issue of such things.

Living harmoniously in the context of others who belong to different generations, cultures, and social classes or who have different educational or professional backgrounds requires of us a certain refinement of behavior. It may well be that newcomers are expected to exhibit a standard of speech, personal hygiene, table

2. Epicetus, *Discourses* 2:10, Great Books (Chicago: Encyclopaedia Britannica, 1952), 149.

manners, punctuality, and ease with customary politeness beyond what was expected of them before entry. With people of their own age and culture, newcomers were previously able to relax and act without much forethought; coming into a mixed community requires a new socialization. This is, obviously, an aspect of formation that cannot be deferred indefinitely—the danger is that any coarseness of manner will cause others in the community to draw back, avoiding contact rather than risking abrasion. It may well be that we expect more of newcomers than we do of veterans—it has sometimes been suggested that a community will tolerate one behavioral oddity for every ten years spent in its midst—perhaps because we want to be sure that a candidate really wants to join the existing community and not to change it into something else.

The basis of friendly relationships in the monastery is the fact of a shared life, *koinos bios*. Years of community experience and of shared goals, and the acceptance of a common tradition and discipline, create a fundamental harmony between brothers or sisters that is able to minimize the effects of the inevitable difficulties of living together. Another factor is also required. Love flourishes to the extent that instinctual behavior is controlled. The greatest obstacles to the growth of love in any relationship are those aspects of life that are ruled by the instincts, which are not subject to the guidance of free, personal decision. Monastic life, because it aims at a degree of freedom from instinctual domination (traditionally termed *apatheia* or purity of heart), creates a climate in which love flourishes naturally and without distortion. The affective life envisaged by Saint Benedict is not so much a sentimental attachment as the disciplined, mature, and non-instinctual desire for the other's good. It is an "ordered" love, *caritas ordinata*, as distinct from the disordinate movements of the passions. This is not to say that it lacks affective warmth and is cool, conceptual, and controlled. It means rather that there is question of *agape* before *eros*, the welfare of the other before self-gratification—be it patent or disguised.

There is always a danger in speaking about love that we will become too eloquent concerning its metaphysical beauty and thereby pay insufficient attention to its practical demands. It is in surfing the ever-changing demands of everyday life in community that character is formed and the virtues developed. On the other hand, a chronic inability to handle the challenges of the common life is usually a sign that a person is in the wrong place and that continuance will more likely lead to vice and unhappiness than to contentment and virtue.

Our participation in community life is impaired, in particular, by three vices that have long been denounced in monastic tradition: *singularitas*, *cupiditas*, *curiositas*. Although they can be named separately, to some extent they overlap and support one another. By identifying the obstacles to sociable living, perhaps we may garner a more precise idea of what needs to be done to achieve this objective. As Saint Jerome remarked, "Things are understood by their opposites."[3]

Singularitas corresponds to what is normally termed "individualism" or, in extreme cases, "solipsism." To the superficial observer it may seem that the monk who habitually indulges in individualistic behavior is enjoying himself in demonstrating some species of superiority over others. There is, however, a dark side to singularity, because often it is no more than a disguised form of passive aggression. By deliberately going my own way, while perhaps feigning inattention to the divergence, I am not only devaluing common norms of conduct, but actively subverting their role in the community. Often there is a less-than-fully-conscious sense of grievance and resentment. I am subtly punishing the community for the unnamable persecution of which I have been a victim. By refusing to conform to common standards I am taking my revenge. Needless to say, such conduct has the effect of increasing the distance between the monk and the community. The alienation becomes greater. This is especially so when lurking behind the grievance is an unacknowledged complicity—the man

3. *Contraria contrariis intelleguntur. Commentarius in Ecclesiasten*, PL 23:1075c.

is, at least, partly responsible for the unhappy situation in which he finds himself though he does not recognize this, and others who dare to suggest this would do so at their peril.

Sometimes another dynamic is operative. A monk who is insecure in his estimation of his own worth may be driven to be demonstrably better than others. He is always ready to go not only the extra mile, but an extra two miles. It is as though he were always trying to prove to others and to himself that he is better than he feels himself to be. In this case his singular fervor is probably an expression of desperate ambition, more driven by forces unrecognized by himself than by the relatively simple desire to improve his standing. We have every reason to look askance at singular behavior because, almost always, there is more to it than meets the eye.

For Bernard, the common life was such a great dynamic for spiritual growth that any recession from it was almost certainly a recipe for disaster:

> They clearly went astray and missed the way of truth when they went back into a solitude of pride. They did not want a social life because singularity cannot have companions. They were in a waterless place, not touched by any rain of tears, a sterile land that is dying because of a permanent and burning dryness.[4]

The fundamental delusion in singularity is that while thinking we belong to ourselves, we allow ourselves to be taken over by a demon. In modern terms this means that although we believe ourselves to be autonomous and to be acting spontaneously, the reality is that we are motivated by unconscious drives. In making ourselves the ultimate determinant of action (*lex sui*) we separate ourselves from God and from love, and we precipitate ourselves into a state where sin is inevitable. Even without overt rebellion

4. Bernard of Clairvaux, PP 1.4; SBOp 5:190.

we have alienated ourselves from God's will and from any prospect of progress in prayer. The relationship with God is impaired if not completely ruptured. As this relationship is weakened, self-destructive behavior increases. Searching for happiness and pleasure apart from God leads only to misery. *Lex sui*, the state of submitting to no outside authority, is the result of self-will; obviously, it blinds itself to the rights, desires, and sufferings of others.[5] Although it may seek to tyrannize others by imposing its rule on them, isolation and alienation will inevitably follow. Seeking to be superior to others, individualists continually assert themselves at the expense of the common life, the common rule, and the common obedience and, not surprisingly, find themselves somewhat excluded from the common affection. Singularity is a disorder: it sets aside the order willed by God; it fails to practice the *ordinatio caritatis* that is at the heart of monastic asceticism. It is a sin against communion, and it becomes a source of division and disharmony in the community.

Community living becomes especially difficult in those cultures in which individualism takes the form of exceptionalism: "I am different, and I need to be treated differently." During the Covid-19 pandemic there were people who refused to self-isolate or wear a mask on the basis that they are "sovereign citizens," a status that they claim exempts them from any external regulation. Most members of monastic communities don't usually go that far, but a

5. That singularity is rampant in monasteries is suggested by Professor Michael Hochschild after a prolonged exploration of several European monasteries: "A perfectly average monk constantly strives after a maximum of self-determination and at the same time for a minimum of determination by others. This means that every monk would prefer to be his own boss, and where this is not possible—as in community life—the potential for conflict arises. An outside observer would expect to find humility and obedience in monastic life, but too often, in reality, individual autonomy and self-fulfillment are paramount. In all monasteries, the values associated with these latter attitudes are markedly higher than the average in society" ("Benediktiner zwischen Kontinuität und Wandel," *Erbe und Auftrag* 89, no. 1 [2013]: 33).

strong sense of entitlement makes community living difficult. It multiplies demands made on common resources and receives from the community with no sense of gratitude or indebtedness. Any failure to meet expectations or any negative impact from others serves to feed a sense of victimhood in which individuals glory in their grievances and carry with them such a long list of wrongs done that they condemn themselves to years of joylessness.[6] Meanwhile their conscience is paralyzed, since in their own thinking, whatever imperfections may exist in their own lives are simply the result of being mistreated or neglected by others.[7] It is no surprise to find that those afflicted by this condition are remarkably skilled at finding pretexts for casting all blame for their unhappiness on the actions or omissions of others. They themselves are paragons of innocence.

The practical effects of *singularitas* are described by Eva Carlotta Rava as the following:

6. "To be a victim is a failure of intelligence. One becomes responsible for one's own life, however difficult that may be. No matter what happens to you, no matter how depressing the material, if it becomes depressing to write, or indeed, to read, it's no good. I firmly believe that unless a thing is understood it is useless, and that the understanding of it is a kind of joy" (John McGahern, interviewed by Sean O'Hagan [for *The Observer*] in *The Age,* October 22, 2005, Review, 3). Joseph Brodsky had this to say at a commencement address at the University of Michigan in 1988: "At all costs try to avoid granting yourselves the status of the victim . . . . No matter how abominable your condition may be, try not to blame anything or anybody: history, the state, superiors, race, parents, the phase of the moon, childhood, toilet training, etc. . . . The moment that you place blame somewhere, you undermine your resolve to change anything" (quoted by J. C. in TLS 6023 [7 September 2018], 36).

7. See Albert Camus, *The Fall* (Harmondsworth: Penguin Books, 1963), 60–61: "We are all exceptional cases. We all want to appeal against something! Each of us insists on being innocent at all cost, even if he has to accuse the whole human race and heaven itself. . . . The essential thing is that they should be innocent, that their virtues, by grace of birth, should not be questioned and that their misdeeds, born of a momentary misfortune, should never be more than provisional."

1. We are unfeeling and uncompassionate about others' sufferings,

2. we have no interest in the common good,

3. we have a tendency to construct our own glory on others' ruin,

4. we desire to leapfrog others in our eagerness to get ahead,

5. we constantly affirm our superiority over others, and

6. we are more concerned with appearances than with reality.[8]

When the effects of *singularitas* are expressed thus we can easily see why singularity and unhappiness are often associated.

Cupiditas is more than covetousness or acquisitiveness. "Cupidity is when you love anything outside God or outside the neighbor, [loved] for God's sake."[9] Replacing the desire that carries us towards God with a multiplicity of desires for temporal benefits results in deep discontent, a lack of progress, and a cumulative deadening of spiritual sensibility. The result is a soul that no longer stands upright but is bent over toward the earth, *anima curva*.[10] The perversion of nature that is *cupiditas* involves the misuse of temporal goods, which, instead of helping us to serve God and neighbor, are seized upon to fill the infinite void within us that cries out for God. Of course, these many desires can never be entirely satisfied and, as a result, quickly become self-replicative. As Ethan notes in John Steinbeck's book *The Winter of Our Discontent,*

---

8. Eva Carlotta Rava, *Caída del hombre y retorna a la verdad en los primeros tratados de San Bernardo de Claraval* (Buenos Aires: EDUCA, 1986), 105.

9. Aelred of Rievaulx, Sermon 46.3; CCCM 2a:366: "The main corrosive influences on fraternal love are cupidity, envy, and suspicion. These are like dying flies that destroy the fragrance of an ointment" (see Eccl 10:1). See also *Sermones* 117.11; CCCM 2c:186.

10. See Michael Casey, *Athirst for God: Spiritual Desire in Bernard of Clairvaux's Sermons on the Song of Songs,* CS 77 (Kalamazoo, MI: Cistercian Publications, 1988), 145–46.

"There is no such thing as just enough money. Only two measures: No Money and Not Enough Money."[11] It is to be noted that in monastic life we do not have to worry much about money, since provision is made for our needs and most of our wants. Our cupidity is directed towards immaterial benefits, employments, official positions, promotions, reputation, honors, privileges. In such cases cupidity may be less visible, but it is still energetically active.

The problem with cupidity is not that there is something necessarily wrong or disordered in the things we seek, nor in the use of them. The poison derives from within ourselves, from a heart turned aside from its proper end to spend its energies in the pursuit of what can never ease its restlessness. As desires multiply, inner unity is weakened, and disintegration sets in at the level of the heart. From there it is just a short step to damaging the unity of the community. In his conference on friendship, John Cassian quotes Abba Joseph as saying, "If [a monk] claims nothing for himself, he entirely cuts off the first cause of quarrels."[12] One who has radically restrained the urgency of *cupiditas* is far more likely to have a positive influence on community life and to live in peace and concord.

Curiositas is more than curiosity or inquisitiveness; it is a matter of expending care on things that are insubstantial, *vanitates*. Saint Bernard is clear on its dangers: "An appetite for vanity is a contempt for the truth, and contempt for the truth is the cause of our blindness."[13] "What does it help you to hold to the truth in your mind while you still hold to vanity in your way of life?"[14] Ultimately, over-concern with things that do not matter leads to a forgetfulness of self, thence to a forgetfulness of God, and, ultimately, to complete estrangement from God.

11. (New York: Penguin, 1996), 112.
12. John Cassian, *Conferences*, 16.6; SCh 54:228.
13. Bernard of Clairvaux, Ep 18:1; SBOp 7:67.
14. Bernard of Clairvaux, Ep 440; SBOp 8:418.

Curiositas is a manifestation of boredom resulting from a failure to take seriously the opportunities of everyday life. It takes many forms, from Cassian's depiction of a monk afflicted with acedia to more contemporary compulsions to seek entertainment and to spend hours on social media or reading newspapers. Galand of Reigny, a contemporary of Saint Bernard, puts the following words in the mouth of a monk afflicted with acedia:

> I seek to occupy the time by any kind of conversation. If I did not pass the day chatting and meandering around I would die of boredom (*taedium*) . . . . To keep silent is a torment, to stay in one place tires me out. Working with my hands was never my thing. Much speaking feeds me, sleep delights me, and I am helped by bodily or mental wandering. I consider myself blessed when I hear rumors or see new things. Every day I would wish for a change of government, new laws, different regulations, so that I might get some relief from boredom from all these variations. I hate whatever lasts a long time, and I draw back in horror from whatever remains the same.[15]

Leap over eight centuries and Jean-Charles Nault offers a more contemporary analysis of a similar state:

> The culture of death is simultaneously a culture dominated by the notion of "entertainment." . . . The very notion of entertainment presumes the state of boredom as the norm, which means that a culture increasingly fueled by this notion assumes that our lives are innately and intrinsically meaningless without the constant stream of "stimulation" and distraction.[16]

15. Galand of Reigny, *Parables* 16.7; SCh 378:228, 230.

16. Jean-Charles Nault, "Acedia: Enemy of Spiritual Joy," *Communio* 31 (Summer 2004): 240. See also Michael Casey, *Strangers to the City: Reflections on the Beliefs and Values of the Rule of Saint Benedict* (Brewster, MA: Paraclete, 2005), 38–44.

Acedia, in its several forms, not only allows any residual spiritual energy to drain away; it renders difficult the task of building community. This is because it opens the door to a great deal of idle conversation, which, in turn, often leads to gossip and detraction. This is especially so when there are discrete groups or factions in a community; when like gathers with like there is a tendency to launch into the bad-mouthing of those who do not belong to the clique, and divisions become ever more irresistibly entrenched.

These are overt vices. There are other underground activities that undermine solidarity in the community but are more or less invisible and are unlikely to be called out by visitators. Unintegrated sexuality not only leads to behavior inconsistent with monastic vows, but it also impedes the blossoming of genuine affection, or causes it to find deviant routes to express itself. Extremes of attachment to or detachment from one or many others in the community are usually signs of persons unduly influenced by a confused sexuality. The occasional appearance of couples and clusters need not necessarily involve overt sexual activity but will almost certainly undermine the community's coherence. That, no doubt, is why Saint Benedict forbids both patronage (taking another under one's wing, RB 69.1) and persecution (striking or excommunicating another, RB 70.2); both are probably indications that some kind of unacknowledged sexual energy is at work.

Other underground activities that invisibly disrupt the harmony of community life include alcohol, tobacco, and drug abuse, internet gambling, clandestine exits from the monastery, secret assignations, fine wining and dining, pornography, and long hours spent on newspapers, social media, and surfing the internet. Since some of these activities require money, creative book-keeping is then called upon to cover a multitude of sins.[17] These are not merely private vices—reprehensible, surely, but nothing to do

---

17. In one community, certain extracurricular activities were entered in the books as "petrol." When the visitator came to inspect the books, he noticed a particularly high amount spent on "petrol" on one occasion. He did some

with anyone else. They have an impact on all. They are like termites that gnaw away at the structure of community life and, if left unchecked, may well lead to disaster.

Although sociability is a by-product of human nature, its operation is often curtailed by these vices. When that happens the quality of community life is degraded. Reversing the situation, however, is not impossible. Beyond the gradual elimination of the more heinous vices, mostly all it takes is the persevering practice of the everyday virtues that Pope Francis recommends: politeness, good humor, helpfulness, and forgiveness. "Love is acquired through the practice of sociability."[18]

We can help the community upgrade by facilitating its growth in love. We can do this simply by making ourselves a little more lovable, so that others don't have to exercise heroic virtue to like us. This is a point made by Saint Bernard, deliberately inverting a well-known quotation of Saint Augustine. If we make ourselves more lovable, we will be more loved, and we will probably find it easier to love in return. We do this by being available, treating people well, and not being unduly disturbed by their infirmities or their misconduct. Thus the total measure of love in the community is increased.

> You will live sociably if you have a zeal *to be loved* and to love, to show yourself as pleasant and accessible, to support not only patiently but gladly the weaknesses of your brothers, their weaknesses both of behavior and of body. [Emphasis added.][19]

---

arithmetic and calculated that the expenditure was sufficient to criss-cross the country several times. No wonder he queried the entry.

18. Bernard of Clairvaux, Div 64.2; SBOp 6a:297.

19. Bernard of Clairvaux, PP 1.4; SBOp 5:190.

Bernard is insistent that we present a pleasant face to those with whom we live. This is probably the counterpart of Pope Francis's exhortations that we avoid presenting as a "sourpuss." "Love is maintained and increased by a friendly expression, a pleasant word, a cheerful deed."[20]

> Because you are placed in a community you are to give precedence to the things that others want over the things that you want. In this way, you will remain among the brothers not only without quarrels but also pleasantly, bearing all and praying for all.[21]

In other words, the practice of ordinary sociability will lead us to love. We do not begin the journey to perfect charity by an effusive affection inflicted on all comers. We begin with civility, courtesy, politeness, respect. In ordinary circumstances, we do not seek to overwhelm the other by our disproportionate love, but to allow mutual affection to grow step by step, as it were, naturally. To make ourselves noticeably more loving than the other is to elevate ourselves into a position of superiority and, thereby, subtly to belittle the other person. Our "love" will probably not be welcomed.

In most communities, the care of the sick and senescent and the welcoming of strangers are covered by official structures. The conduct of those who are immediately involved is prescribed by Saint Benedict. They are to be diligent and caring, showing to those for whom they are responsible the same concern that they would extend to Christ, were he in that situation. For the rest of us, care of the old and sick will be more informal and will often depend on our past relationship. Above all, it is important that we treat others respectfully as normal adults and not infantilize them—as carers sometimes do. Physical frailty or hearing loss do not make people stupid. If dementia begins to appear we adjust

---

20. Bernard of Clairvaux, Div 121; SBOp 6a:399.
21. Bernard of Clairvaux, Nat 3.6; SBOp 4:216.

our relationship, but we patiently maintain our respect and love, and try to meet them wherever they are. We are still bound by the obligations of communal solidarity, even though the forms it takes may have to be radically different.

Sociability depends to a large extent on conversation. Notwithstanding the age-old tradition of inculcating silence, friendly conversation is one of the six means of monastic formation listed by the thirteenth-century Cistercian Adam of Perseigne.[22] Certainly Saint Teresa of Ávila seems to have been in no doubt about the importance of recreation in adding balance and sustainability to a contemplative community.[23] Here we have to be somewhat imaginative. Adult encounter is not the same as the idle chatter rejected by so many monastic legislators. It is a means of consolidation of relationship, not merely the passing of time or the communication of information. This conversation implies a mutual presence or hospitality, the giving of time and space to another. In a world devoted to fake news and trivialities, the importance of serious conversation cannot be ignored. Adult dialogue is not only a means of attaining a fuller human maturity but also an essential instrument of evangelization in a pluralistic world.

22. Adam of Perseigne, Ep 5.55; SCh 66:118.

23. Father Terrence Kardong is of the same mind. See his article "Monastic Recreation," in *Tjurunga* 74 (2008): 73–80. With regard to the Strict Observance Cistercians, the 1924 Constitutions contained the sentence, "There is no recreation in Houses of the Order." At the 1984 General Chapter an attempt was made to include a similar proposition in the revised Constitutions. This was defeated by one vote (*Minutes*, 313). An attempt by the Promoter of the General Chapter, Dom André Louf, to retake the vote was blocked on procedural grounds. Later a vote was taken giving an authentic interpretation of the rejection of the proposal: "We do not wish to introduce this amendment as it is into our Constitutions. The sense of this vote is not: 'We wish to modify the present practice of the Order in this area.'" This was accepted 81-4 (*Minutes*, 388). The matter was not discussed by the 1985 General Chapter of Abbesses nor by the 1987 Mixed General Meeting. Mysteriously, however, the 1924 text was inserted after the text was approved by the Chapter and before it was submitted to the Holy See. It was appended to Statute 24A, where it remains to this day.

The Christian Church is best understood as a schooling in conversation. Such a schooling is necessary because truthful converse requires the recognition that the "self" who speaks must first be heard by others in order to be a self at all. It requires that I recognize others as themselves constitutive of my own identity. To be a self requires a mutuality of trust that permits the risk of recognizing my inescapable interdependence on others. In order to find myself, I must dispossess myself.[24]

Note how challenging authentic conversation is. It requires a lot of self-restraint so that the ego is silenced and room is left for the other person to fill. My identity is confirmed in serious interchange, but I must first be prepared to create space so that it can happen. The main obstacles to fruitful conversation are lack of leisure, overwork, lack of patience, excessive search for entertainment, competitiveness, ambition, and long-lasting animosities based on real or imagined sources of grievance. This means that we should have as our ideal "to bring to all conversation and discussion a tranquil spirit, a firmness, and a friendliness that will eliminate bitterness or irritation from the opponent's mind."[25] This means avoiding the expansion of long-term resentments such as those persons experience who feel that they are unfairly marginalized or excluded from participating in administrative decisions. Even when they don't complain, they are hurt when they are not kept informed or when they are never consulted, even in matters in which they have a certain expertise. As Harold Macmillan remarked, it is not easy to find oneself powerless in a group to which one has dedicated oneself: "A man ought perhaps to enjoy a balanced and genial temperament to withstand the temptations of a non-executive post. An active and diligent man can

24. Gerard Loughlin, reviewing Rowan Williams' *On Christian Theology*, in *Times Literary Supplement*, 4 August 2000.

25. Elizabeth Leseur (1866–1914); quoted in *Give Us This Day*, 25 April 2017.

easily be tempted into criticising and interfering with his colleagues or framing large but unrealistic plans."[26]

A particular aspect of verbal interchange between community members is a willingness to offer praise when something is well done. Saint Augustine includes this quality among the characteristic actions of friends: we praise them when they do well. In many communities such mutual praise can be relatively rare, inhibited by envy, competitiveness, ill-will, or inertia. We sometimes forget that when others do well it is usually because they have been diligent and generous in producing the desired result.[27] It is more than good luck.

A lot of self-restraint is required to maintain a sincere level of geniality when the circumstances of daily life become uncomfortable or distasteful or when every day is unutterably the same. Continuing to flourish in such a situation requires a whole array of qualities, particularly humility and its cousin humor. Genuine humility gives birth to an important triad of virtues that not only secures our own inner contentment but is an important element in guaranteeing the peace and harmony of the community. We can scarcely overestimate the importance of three overlapping attitudes:

26. Harold Macmillan, *The Blast of War: 1939–1945* (London: Macmillan, 1967), 181–82. He is speaking of Sir Stafford Cripps.

27. We need to be aware that praise can also be part of a system of sanctions intended to reinforce power. To praise is to reward: to withhold praise is to punish: "It is called praise. It is supposed to be a small act of kindness. Next time she came past, and was right behind you, you could feel the fear from the one she had praised. Not a big fear, physical punishment did not come into it. But a subtle, little fear that would only be obvious to someone who had never received much in the way of praise. The fear of not being as good as last time; of not being worthy this time as well. You knew that, always, when Karin Ærø came up behind you, so too came a judge" (Peter Høeg, *Borderliner* [London: The Harvill Press, 1996], 46). Praise can be an example of what Saint Benedict condemns as patronage (RB 69), a means of keeping another in a subservient position. And we need to be aware that flattery of the powerful is not sincere praise. As Seneca noted, "Even a low-born peasant / can get true praise. But only the powerful / can get false praise" (spoken by Atreus in *Thyestes* Act II:210–12).

a. To be non-reactive,

b. to be non-assertive, and

c to be non-judgmental.[28]

I will be happier if I refuse to others the power to dictate how I feel. I do this by breaking the nexus between the words, actions, and omissions of another and my own instinctual reaction. If I become a more thoughtful person, who has the power to step back from an unpleasant situation until such times as emotions are stilled, I will find a way to craft a response that is worthy of me and does no harm to another. Besides, if somebody is deliberately trying to provoke me, they will be frustrated by my calm demeanor and will probably be a little less likely to continue to stir me.

There are occasions in which self-assertion is both useful and necessary, but there are many other situations in which it is wiser to step back and not intervene. John Macquarrie insists that love for others is not always a matter of coming closer or seeking friendship; sometimes it is expressed by giving other persons as much space as they need as they advance toward a fuller humanity. Love can be a deliberate standing back in order to allow others to find their freedom. It is not an absence of care or concern but selfless desire that the other person may grow. This sometimes includes allowing them to make mistakes, in the hope that the experience will be more instructive than mere hectoring on our part: "Most typically, 'letting-be' means helping a person into the full realization of his potentialities for being":[29]

28. These attitudes govern the way that I act. It is also important that I ensure that the way I respond to the actions of others is not toxic. This means that I take steps to recognize and diminish the first movements of resentment and envy; these vices are sometimes more difficult to discern.

29. "This is so because love, in its ontological sense, is letting-be. Love usually gets defined in terms of union, or the drive toward union, but such a definition is too egocentric. Love does indeed lead to community, but to aim primarily at uniting the other person to oneself, or oneself to him, is not the

Richard Sennett speaks about interacting in the subjunctive mood, relinquishing all claims to infallibility (however well justified), and seasoning one's conversations with such words as "perhaps," "maybe," and "It seems to me." We should bear in mind the conclusions of the Dunning-Kruger study that found an inverse correlation between confidence and competence. Those who are truly competent in some field tend to talk about it with a degree of tentativeness. Those who are not competent are, too often, boisterously confident in their own knowledge and prowess. Overemphasis is often a disguise for uncertainty. In addition, dominating the conversation by speaking loudly, by being too dogmatic, or by engaging in self-pleasing monologues does nothing to enhance cohabitation. The patience of many communities is as stretched to breaking point by the bombast of those who are always right as also by the constant drone of resident bores, who never say in ten words what can be said in a thousand. To check the quality of community life it is worth monitoring the quality of conversation.

The social engine is oiled when people do not behave too emphatically. The subjunctive mood is most at home in the

---

secret of love and may even be destructive of genuine community. Love is letting-be, not of course in the sense of standing off from someone or something, but in the positive and active sense of enabling-to-be. When we talk of 'letting-be,' we are to understand both parts of this hyphenated expression in a strong sense— 'letting' as 'empowering,' and 'be' as enjoying the maximal range of being that is open to the particular being concerned. Most typically, 'letting-be' means helping a person into the full realisation of his potentialities for being; and the greatest love will be costly, since it will be accomplished by the spending of one's own being. Love is letting-be even when this may demand the loosening of the bonds that bind the beloved person to oneself; this might well be the most costly of demands, and it is in the light of this kind of love that drive toward union may seem egocentric. . . . The Christian religion affirms that 'God is love' and this is so because love is letting-be, and we have seen that the very essence of God as being is to let-be, to confer, sustain, and perfect the being of the creatures" (John Macquarrie, *Principles of Christian Theology*, rev. ed. [London: SCM Press, 1977], 348–49).

dialogical domain, that world of talk which makes an open space, where discussion can take an unforeseen direction. . . . By practising indirection, speaking to one another in the subjunctive mood, we can experience a certain kind of sociable pleasure: being with other people, focusing on and learning about them, without forcing ourselves into the mould of being like them.[30]

Perhaps we do not give enough emphasis to the contribution made by restraint in speech, especially by being fully in control of what issues forth from our mouth. Reducing the amount of uncharitable discussion makes possible a comfortable silence that can contribute much to the warmth of affective community as also to the quality of eventual conversation.

Refusing to engage in rash judgment of others will be a lifelong struggle for many of us. As soon as we embrace an ideal of appropriate behavior and invest energy and effort in approaching it, we begin to notice that others are not so engaged by the values that we have adopted. To bolster our wavering will, we begin to make comparisons between ourselves and others, arriving at an appraisal that is generally in our own favor. Anyone who has ever tried to lose weight by eating less will probably remember how aware they became of the unbridled eating habits of others. It is as though it is very difficult for us to practice virtue without being condemnatory of the way that others act who, perhaps, dedicate themselves more fully to different values and virtues.

It is easy to be critical of the lack of virtue we see around us. We can also be dismissive of those who are zealous in areas where we tend to be easygoing. Sometimes, it is true, this punctiliousness can be obsessive or compulsive behavior, but it can also be earnestness and fervor in putting into practice the beliefs and values that we ourselves commonly praise but generally do not bother about.

---

30. Richard Sennett, *Together: The Rituals, Pleasures and Politics of Cooperation* (New Haven: Yale University Press, 2005), 23.

If we are honest we may become aware that, in reality, we are resentful of those whose fidelity puts our own mediocrity to shame.

One part of the remedy for reactiveness, assertiveness, and being judgmental is learning the art of minding our own business and not being preoccupied with what other people are doing. It is easier said than done. Saint Aelred was aware of this:

> There is no doubt that those who take their eyes off themselves, being unwilling to pay attention to themselves, that is, to their own weakness, but preferring to examine the lives of others and pass judgment on them, depart from their membership of Christ's flock and [instead] feed their own carnal senses with wicked and sinful delight.[31]

There is a great advantage in simply getting on with one's own work and one's own life, bearing the idiocies of others when they impinge on us, and not neglecting to make intercession for those among whom we live. This means that, following the Lord's commandment, we pray especially for those whom we may sometimes qualify as our enemies.

A second part of the remedy is growing in our capacity for forgiveness, that is to say, deliberately developing the ability to let go of the memories that disturb us and cause estrangement from others.[32] We do not have to approve the misdeeds of others;

31. Aelred of Rievaulx, Sermon 3:21; CCCM 2A:31.

32. The memory plays a large part in how we feel. It can make us aggrieved even when there is nothing negative currently affecting us. The memory of wrongs done evokes in us an emotive response that is sometimes stronger than that generated by the original incident. "Now a most powerful and complex part of the personality is affection, and affection springs straight out of the memory." Thus John B. Yeats writes to his son W. B. Yeats. See Colm Tóibín, *Mad, Bad, Dangerous to Know: The Fathers of Wilde, Yeats and Joyce* (London: Viking, 2018), 100. The relationship between peace and memory is graphically presented in Kazuo Ishiguro's novel *The Buried Giant.* Axl and Beatrice and, indeed, the entire population, are able to live peaceably because collective memory has been disabled. As it begins to return, the capacity for peaceful coexistence is fractured.

we do not have to enjoy them. We will be much happier, however, if we do not allow them to dominate our thoughts and arouse negative feelings in us. Above all, we do not permit their perceived offenses to lead us into uncharity. We have to learn the skill of remaining somewhat aloof from the inner disturbance that harsh treatment inevitably generates.[33]

A third part of the remedy is to grow in understanding. First, to refrain from condemning the other person outright, but to try to appreciate some of the factors that may have contributed to their actions. Second, to make an effort to read the negative situation with a little more objectivity. Third, to try to assess the contribution made by one's own actions and not to shy away from the admission of some degree of complicity on one's own part.

Effective and affective community is not only a pleasant place in which to live. Mutual encouragement stimulates creativity. A vibrant community will be one in which different talents are recognized, appreciated, promoted, and utilized. This increases the sense of well-being among the members, and it also means that the community has more to contribute to the church and to the world. Unaffirmed talents swiftly degenerate to the point of

---

Since memory is dependent on the frequency and recency of recollection, the ability deliberately to dismiss intrusive memories is an important means of resisting conditioning by the past. As such, it is a useful tool for community living.

33. I have discussed aspects of forgiveness in *Seventy-Four Tools for Good Living: Reflections on the Fourth Chapter of Benedict's Rule* (Collegeville, MN: Liturgical Press, 2014), 76–83, 102–14, 241–43. See especially 243. "In a sermon preached three weeks before being kidnapped, Father Christian de Chergé summarized his approach to peacemaking in five words. 'There are five pillars of peace: Patience, poverty, presence, prayer and pardon.' These are elements on which we could profitably meditate when we find ourselves in a situation where peace is threatened or concord disturbed. To endure suffering, to be willing to go without, never to break a relationship, to pray for those who may have offended us, and to let go of our grievances. Learning to live thus on a daily basis will ensure that we will, in truth, return to peace as soon as possible with those with whom we have quarreled or with whom we have had a disagreement or a difference."

undermining the cohesion of the group. On the other hand, an array of discerned and affirmed talents operating in harmony builds up a culture within the community that can form newcomers to continue the charism. Too many malcontents in a community renders this unlikely.

Cultures represent distinct essays at integration of all the real components of concrete social life. When some progress is made toward rationality, local talent and local products combine to generate a unique, local blend of social living. If the society is whole enough to encourage innovation, talented individuals emerge from its midst with visions and plans for a specific and higher form of integration. Advances in art, religion, government, cooking, amusement, and science can result from one person's fresh insight. This insight is not, however, to be regarded as an individualistic triumph. The best advances are ingenious integrations of accumulations of beliefs/values already present in the society. Individuals are the organs of association and co-ordination, not the discoverers of a new star. They bring forth from the existing culture something of its hidden potential. On the other hand, the best advance is often that which everyone believes themselves to have known all along, lacking only the capacity to formulate it. Cultural advance is a social event. Individuals of greater insight/vision/skill create around them others who collectively extend and apply their teaching. A tradition is begun in which something of the full potential of the innovation is spun out through the subsequent ages. In the emergence and perdurance of culture, nothing is more important than the involvement of talented individuals. When a society becomes repressive, culture becomes moribund.

The strength of a society's culture is the measure of the strength of the commitment of individuals to the society. In a situation of cultural erosion, old loyalties fail, and divergent channels of influence offset the possibility of revival. Individuals no longer identify with the society; their modes of expressing their personal nature and needs no longer coincide with those proposed to them by the society for this purpose. A strong culture, on the other hand, forges strong social bonds. No further reward is required for adherence to what is beautiful.

Culture is not the prerogative of the sophisticated, nor is it to be confounded with the manners (and affectations) of genteel society. It is fundamentally the humanity that characterizes the work that we do, how we interact with others, and how we allow ourselves to become vehicles of inspiration and innovation in our own environment.

Perhaps we need to be convinced that working to make our monastic community a living witness to Gospel values is the first step towards realizing the mission entrusted to us. If onlookers say of us in all sincerity, "See how they love one another," and it is true, then not only are we fulfilling the Lord's precept, but we are also allowing our own intimate lives to become a sacrament of evangelization. And what more could be asked of us?

11

Cloistral Paradise

In the fifth century, a Syriac anthology of monastic texts, including Palladius's *Lausiac History*, appeared under the title "The Paradise of the Fathers."[1] The implication such a title conveys is that monastic life is as close to heaven as it is possible to attain on earth. Living in a monastery is to be understood as approaching the frontiers of Paradise.[2]

After the expulsion of Adam and Eve, Paradise remained untended but unchanged. It was still Paradise. It was the culprits who were changed, evicted as they were from their former home. Their life became dominated by shame, labor, and pain. Created in God's image, they had through their rebellion lost their likeness to God, and, because of that, their lives were marked by misery. Death lurked just around the corner. To those mourning and weeping in this valley of tears, heaven seemed a distant prospect. Alienated from God and dwelling in this region of unlikeness (*regio*

---

1. English translation by Ernest A. Wallis Budge, *The Paradise or Garden of the Holy Fathers: Being Histories of the Anchorites, Recluses, Monks, Coenobites, and Ascetic Fathers of the Deserts of Egypt between A.D. CCL and A.D. CCCC circiter* (London: Chatto & Windus, 1907).

2. This is the title of a book by Peter Levi, *Frontiers of Paradise: A Study of Monks and Monasteries* (London: Collins Harvill, 1987).

dissimilitudinis), they wandered around in circles, unable to break through the walls of their self-chosen exile.

Christians often viewed their task as regaining, by God's grace, the Paradise that had been lost. Especially among North African writers like Cyprian and Augustine, there was a strong sense that we are living in distant exile and must make a long and hazardous journey to reach our homeland. They made their own the words, "Here we have no abiding city, but seek one which is in the future" (Heb 13:14).[3] The journey is made, as Saint Augustine reiterates, not by changing our location but by changing our priorities. It is a matter of re-orienting our affective energies so that we seek the things that are above.

The spirituality that grew from such a stance inevitably placed a great emphasis on desire for God and for eternal life.[4] This in turn demanded the identification and elimination of all those other desires that could serve as substitutes or compensations for this primal yearning. Worldly desires anchor the soul to the sphere of space and time and distract it from the purpose of reaching eternal life in the kingdom of God. They are like the hostile tribes that blocked Israel from reaching the Promised Land. With God's help, these unseen adversaries must be found, faced, fought, and frustrated.

Monastic life avowedly represents an attempt to engage in this spiritual warfare in a systematic and enduring manner. It is meant to be a road to eternal life. The various visible observances that any visitor can notice do not necessarily convey what is at the heart of a monastic vocation. No one in their right mind would choose to spend the rest of their lives under curfew, chirruping psalms, making cheese, and having their lives ruled by the ringing of the bell. There must be some powerful motivating dynamic operating beneath the threshold of what the casual observer can perceive. If the price is so high the value of the product must be immense.

3. Bernard of Clairvaux quotes the text eleven times.
4. See Isabelle Bochet, *Saint Augustin et le désir de Dieu* (Paris: Études Augustiniennes, 1982).

In a sense, it is less a mystery why people enter a monastery than why they stay. Most people who enter monastic life are cushioned by a set of illusions about what they will find when they arrive.[5] Only those stay who are patient until some kind of synthesis is reached between what they hoped for and what they find. Since the community is unlikely to change, this outcome requires us continually to refine our hopes and expectations until a match is made. Perseverance is really a matter of finding in the reality of community life the buried treasure for the purchase of which we sold everything. Sometimes this takes a lot of digging.

The defining feature of monastic life is not the digging but the finding. Oh, yes. Monks and nuns do begin to find what they came for, without the life around them getting more glamorous. Those lucky enough to enter at an advanced age or who die young reach the goal fairly quickly. For the rest of us, our dreams begin to look a little more realistic only once we pass four or five decades. The ups and downs of the intervening years don't much matter. What is important, as Saint Benedict seemed to imply in his notion of stability, is that we stick around and keep trying, undeterred by many inconsistencies and compromises and occasional failures.

We may be able to accept the proposition that monastic life is a road by which we can travel toward heaven, but it strains our credulity to believe that monastic life is already heaven. It feels more like purgatory. A lot depends on how we envisage heaven. If we think of heaven and hell as two distinct places, then they are separated by a vast abyss. The problem is that space and time are features of this world only. The distance between heaven and hell is not geographical; it is subjective. The same reality seems all-glorious to one and utter doom to another.

Imagine you have been given premium tickets to attend Wagner's *Ring Cycle*. Can there be anything more delightful than to be

---

5. "There is nothing in science that says that illusions may not be useful, even indispensable, in life" (John Gray, *Seven Types of Atheism* [London: Allen Lane, 2018], 13).

immersed in sixteen hours of Wagnerian music? Apparently, some do not think so. To them such exposure would be closer to hell than to heaven. In this case, it is not the music that makes the difference; it is the receptivity of the one who hears it. To the damned soul, even the singing of the angelic choirs is a hateful cacophony.

This seems to be saying that beauty is mainly in the eyes of the beholder. As Saint Leo the Great remarked, "Dirty vision cannot see the splendor of the true light; what is joy to minds that are cleansed is punishment to tarnished minds."[6] The work of monastic life then is to clean the windows of the soul so that it becomes possible to be enchanted by what is seen—not only by what will be seen once we arrive in heaven but by what we can perceive even now in this world that is the work of God's hands and that is sustained by divine providence.

So tell me your impressions of the monastic community in which you live, and I will give you a reading of the state of your soul. If you are overcome by admiration for the holy lives lived by others, their giftedness, their magnanimity, then I will conclude that you are a very humble person, very happy, and, for you, monastic life is indeed a paradise. If your assessment of others is a bit grumpier, I suppose it means that you have some distance to travel before you arrive at your goal.

One of the things that prevents most of us from appreciating the value of those with whom we live is the fact that they are different from us. They experience things differently, they think differently, they respond differently. They have a different range of talents and skills and occupy a different position in the community. To the extent that we have installed ourselves as the ultimate norm of all truth, goodness, and beauty, it will seem that others are severely deficient. We find ourselves praying that, by the grace of God, they will become more like us.

6. Leo the Great, Sermon 95.8; PL 54:466b. *Merito haec beatitudo cordis promittitur puritati. Splendorem enim veri luminis sordens acies videre non poterit: et quod erit iucunditas mentibus nitidis hoc erit poena maculosis.*

Unlike us, Saint Bernard was inclined to celebrate differences between members of the community as testimony to the powerfully unitive force of the monastic vocation. It seems that no two monks were pursuing identical ways to God; each was following a particular path:

> The monastery is truly a paradise, a region fortified with the ramparts of discipline. It is a glorious thing to have men living together in the same house following the same way of life. How good and how pleasant it is when brothers live in unity. You will see one of them weeping for his sins, another rejoicing in the praise of God, another tending the needs of all, while another is giving instruction to the rest. Here is one who is at prayer and another at reading; here is one who is compassionate and another who inflicts penalties for sins. This one is aflame with love, and that one is valiant in humility. This one remains humble when everything goes well, and this other one does not lose his nerve in difficulties. This one works very hard in active tasks, the other finds quiet in the practice of contemplation.[7]

If we take Bernard's lyrical depiction of heaven as a program toward which a community must work, then a monastery will be characterized by delight, brilliance, happiness, completion, sweetness, peace, satisfaction, and vision.[8] Not all monasteries of my acquaintance fully meet that expectation, but most of them are trying.

It is to be hoped that monastic communities present some evidence that the Last Things are in process of realization,[9] for "a holy

---

7. Bernard of Clairvaux, Div 42.4; SBOp 6/1:258.

8. Bernard of Clairvaux, Div 42.7, SBOp 6a:260–61; SC 33.2, SBOp 1:234; Dil 33, SBOp 3:147.

9. If you prefer: monastic life is an example of *sich realisierende Eschatologie*. See Michael Casey, *Athirst for God: Spiritual Desire in Bernard of Clairvaux's*

soul is, itself, a heaven."[10] Apart from a burgeoning unanimity, the other manifestations of progress in this direction include what Saint Bernard terms "the paradise of a good conscience," whereby the consequence of conscientious living is a deep peace in which the trials and turmoil of earth are relativized.[11] And since from the abundance of the heart the mouth speaks, one living on the threshold of heaven is known by their wisdom, which Saint Bernard considered to be the effect of the outshining of eternal light, *candor lucis aeternae*.[12] Above all, it is the experience of being drawn into the "third heaven," like Saint Paul, that indicates that if the monk has not already arrived, at least he has one foot inside the gates.[13] Ecstasy or *excessus* is an advanced experience of self-transcendence that may be considered an experiential foretaste of the heavenly life.[14] Even though the experience is fleeting it portends an eternity of bliss:

> What is to be said of those who are sometimes snatched away by the Spirit through the self-transcendence of contemplation, and who are thus able to experience something of the sweetness of heavenly joy? Do they experience this freedom from unhappiness (*libertas a miseria*) as often as this takes place? It is not to be denied that these, though they are still in the flesh, do enjoy the liberty of bliss (*libertas complaciti*), though the experience is rare and very brief. They, like Mary, have chosen the better part, and it shall not be taken from them. Those who in the present hold on to

---

Sermons on the Song of Songs, CS 77 (Kalamazoo, MI: Cistercian Publications, 1988), 290–98.

10. Bernard of Clairvaux, SC 27.8; SBOp 1:187.

11. See Casey, *Athirst for God*, 282–87.

12. See Casey, *Athirst for God*, 296–98.

13. *In momentaneum hoc, latet aeternitas.* Bernard of Clairvaux, "In this momentary experience heaven hides" (QH 17.3; SBOp 4:488).

14. See Michael Casey, "In Pursuit of Ecstasy: Reflections on Bernard of Clairvaux's *De Diligendo Deo*," *Monastic Studies* 16 (1985): 139–56.

what is not to be taken from them certainly experience what is future. And what is future is happiness, and since happiness and unhappiness cannot coexist, therefore, when the Spirit allows them to share such happiness, then they enjoy the liberty of bliss, even though this is a partial experience, very deficient relative to the full experience, and also exceeding rare.[15]

What happens during the high moments of prayer is not a change in a person's status before God, but the experiential revelation to the person of the ongoing truth of graced human being. Time and eternity are not separated; space-time exists within eternity. I exist in time within eternity. That is why what I do in time has eternal significance. That is why monks and nuns who allow themselves to be formed by the grace of the Gospel see things differently, evaluate things differently, and are themselves . . . different.

Viewing monastic life—and, indeed, all Christian life—as an initiation into the life of heaven may seem over-poetic and unrealistic. What we see around us and what we experience every day seems to us quite unlike what we may expect to find in heaven. So it seems to us. But perhaps this is because our perception is deficient. What we have in this community is the handiwork of God's creation arranged by divine providence. If there is imperfection—as there certainly is—it is only because the work is still in process. What causes us so much distaste is only temporary until its purpose is served. And who knows? Perhaps that purpose is to allow us to develop a longer vision and a broader compassion. When that work is done, the imperfection will fade away.

The reality is more than a metaphor. Because the monastery is an ecclesial community, it is marked with the seal of mystery. There is more going on than meets the eye. Yes, it is a collection of mediocre men or women going about their business, living in a situation that is ordinary, obscure, and laborious, but with an

15. Bernard of Clairvaux, Gra 15; SBOp 3:177.

eye often cast upwards, with a secret sense of the presence of Christ and a growing familiarity with the Communion of Saints. Unbeknownst to them, life in community is purifying their gaze and unifying their choices. Although faults and foolishnesses remain, they no longer have the power to tarnish what is happening interiorly. A subtle transformation is occurring.

At the end of a lifelong search for God, life becomes very simple, but very intense—because it is concentrated on a single goal. Romano Guardini seems to have thought that if we linger long on the lands bordering Paradise, we begin to live more in eternity than in time, and our thoughts and affections often slip over the frontier, until one day, in a moment of special intensity, we decide to follow them with our whole heart and our whole soul and our whole mind and all our strength:

> But in the case of moral (as distinct from practical) obligation, we are conscious that we touch the Absolute. Utility vanishes once the object is reached. Goodness is permanent . . . it is timeless. And the more a man wills the absolute, the more he himself participates in its character. The more firmly and energetically he strives for the good, the more he grows into the nature of the Absolute—Goodness. Consequently, if a man willed a thing wholly good in itself, and willed it with complete candour and with all his heart, pouring into this willing and doing the full measure of his vital force, a mysterious thing would happen. He would have passed into eternity.[16]

In this moment the goal of our monastic journey has been attained.

---

16. Romano Guardini, *The Last Things* (London: Burns & Oates, 1954), 105. He qualifies this further on (105–6). "Of himself man cannot attain to this state of eternity. His own capacities are insufficient to reach a wholly living present in which goodness is perfectly realized . . . eternity is not ours by nature, though we are directed toward it and long for it. Our participation depends on our relationship with God."

The Nature and Uses of Prayer
by Nedoncelle
(trans., Manson '64)